IRISH FAIRY TALES

IRISH FAIRY TALES

Padraic O'Farrell

Gill & Macmillan

Gill & Macmillan Ltd
Hume Avenue, Park West
Dublin 12
with associated companies throughout the world
www.gillmacmillan.ie

© *Padraic O'Farrell 1997*
978 07171 3168 6

Original text design by
Identikit Design Consultants, Dublin
Illustrations by Peter Jones
Print origination by Carole Lynch
Printed in Malaysia

This book is typeset in 10/15 pt Adobe Garamond.

The paper used in this book comes from the wood pulp
of managed forests. For every tree felled, at least one tree
is planted, thereby renewing natural resources.

A CIP catalogue record for this book is available
from the British Library.

CONTENTS

TO SÍOFRA

INTRODUCTION

A re they the Tuatha Dé Danaan, those tribes of the Celtic goddess, Dana, who retired into the hills of Ireland after their defeat by the Milesians? Are they servants of the gods? Are they the angelic hurlers on the ditch who took neither side in the struggle between the Archangel and Lucifer and who, as a result, must wander this world until the Day of Judgment? Are they evil or good? Do they live in communities or operate alone? In the Land of Youth, Tír na n-Óg, or in ordinary fairy mounds called *liosacháin*. Are they merely devices used by the *seanchaí*, that popular Irish story-teller given to entertaining his neighbours by the fireside with his well-embellished tales? Whatever their origin, the *sidhe*, the good people, the wee folk, the fairies, fill pages of Irish literature as well as enriching a wealth of oral tradition.

Irish scholars have chronicled fairy tales for centuries. Monks in ancient abbeys used stylish calligraphy and artistic diagrams to develop themes of great quests in the Eastern world or hostings in the hearts of Irish hills. Authors like William Carleton, Lady Wilde, W. B. Yeats and Lady Gregory contributed to this corpus. The Kerry playwright, George Fitzmaurice, crammed *The Enchanted Land* with inhabitants of the sea-bed land of Manannan Mac Lir, an Irish version of the sea-god, Neptune. The waves and their wildlife — seals and fish, mermaids and phantom craft — have associations with fairies too. Music and dancing and merriment abounded in some fairy tales. So did feats of horsemanship and of strength, alongside weaknesses, wiles and wantonness. Seldom did the written word equal the effect of the oral narrative. It did, however, present the *seanchaí* with a basic pattern upon which to weave his descriptive tapestry. And how he revelled in his art of embellishment and exaggeration! As one generation passed on its fanciful tales to the next, the basic story remained the same but an added charm came with each retelling.

Country people steeped in superstition sometimes feared the *sidhe*. More often, they enjoyed listening to stories about them. Many doubters played practical jokes on believers. However they might scoff at the same believers, they held in their hearts an acceptance of the possibility of a supernatural existence in the form of fairies. Some families swore that the Banshee (*Bean sidhe*, fairy woman) keened on the night before the death of a member. Others would never build a house between two fairy forts, because the wee folk would be passing that way. When there was a doubt about the fairies' right of way, builders left foundations unfilled for a few nights; if the trenches crossed a fairy pass, the wee folk would fill them in and the builder would choose another site. A returned American defied custom and built on a fairy pass, against all local advice. He held a house warming, a party to celebrate the occupation of the newly built premises. Good spirits prevailed until midnight when bad spirits had their fling in earnest. They flung pots, pans, kettles and assorted earthenware around the house. Then the roof fell in. As revellers scattered, they were buffeted by an unknown force. The piper stopped playing when his mouth went around to the back of his head. A horn protruded from the owner's forehead. By morning, nothing remained of the building. Next day, the owner hurried back to America. Quite recently, a land reclamation scheme ground to a halt as a JCB operator refused to tamper with a fairy fort.

A religious race mingled religion with piseoga (superstitious practices) and uttered an apology or exhortation to the *sidhe* as often as a prayer to God. Parishes had their *bean feasa* (wise woman) or *fear feasa* (wise man). Many of these received their healing powers, it was thought, from the fairies. Only a hundred years ago, a Tipperary farmer burned his young wife to death, believing that the fairies substituted her for the girl he married. Fairies could do good or evil, depending on how mortals treated them.

The Irish spirit of fun nurtured its fairy lore too. Few could deny the foreigner his pleasure of believing that around the next turn of the road might be lurking a leprechaun who would lead him to a crock of gold at the rainbow's end. If they did not, however, they frightened the life out of the same visitor with tall tales of giants and pookas that they would surely meet before their vacation ended. Or about An Fear Gurtha, the hungry man who might cast his hungry grass under their feet and lead them astray on the next leg of their journey. Lonely poets might hear about the Leannán Sidhe, the fairy lover who would seduce them in return for inspiration. (Does modern poetry testify to its extinction?) Perhaps professional babysitters eager to attract business spread the news about the little red man, An Fear Dearg, who stole healthy mortal babies and left sick fairy infants in their place.

Time passed and customs changed. A box in the corner replaced the *seanchaí*. An alleged sophistication spurned simple entertainment. So the great tradition of passing down fairy stories orally is in decline, if not completely extinct. There is, therefore, a need for concise collections of lesser-known tales, told with a contemporary idiom. For example, many of the best-loved stories each took a half-hour or more to tell. If the narrator noticed special interest in some part of his account, he exploited this by dwelling longer on that portion of his story with the next telling. If he had a really rapt audience, his tale could go on for an hour. There was considerable repetition in these stories. Invariably, a young man seeking the hand of a princess in marriage got three tasks to perform. The blueprint story meticulously described identical circumstances for each attempt. The hurly-burly world of sound-bite and Internet surfing that heralds the approach of the twenty-first century would not tolerate that technique.

A pocket edition demands extra brevity. This, however, might prove to be a blessing, because I believe that the very survival of the fairy story demands a more fluid and brief narration than it received previously. I read some of the stories in this collection during my lifetime. I listened to others, sitting by country firesides in many counties of Ireland over half a century, as a child eager for diversion and as an adult researching books on Irish life and lore. I do not retell them here exactly as I read or heard them. Such a narration would not suit the time or the medium. For the reasons stated, I write condensed versions. Like the *seanchaí* of old, however, I have taken the liberty of spicing the original with a little humour, again, with a contemporary readership in mind. I hope the wee folk will understand and permit publication!

ONE

MAUREEN'S CLURICAUN

I n fairy lore, the Cluricaun is a sprite that uses a *buachalán buidhe*, or ragwort, as a steed to get him from one wealthy gentleman's house to the next or from one foxhunting meet to the other. Other branches of the *sidhe* frown upon this habit of hobnobbing with the gentry. Yet they tolerate him, because fairies admire skills in horsemanship and one who can ride a mere weed to overcome the opposition of well-bred pookas and hacks is indeed special. Such a person gains the respect of Fionvara himself, that champion huntsman, with his black stallion whose deep red nostrils breathe fire.

A Roscommon Cluricaun cantered by the shores of Lough Ree on his *buachalán* one fine summer day. He heard the horn of the master of the Galway Blazers who were far from home and searching a covert near by. Hastily, he jumped behind a furze bush and hid until the brightly clad gentry came by. As they did, he joined them. Now, to mere mortals, the Cluricaun and his mount appear as a handsome male on a fine black horse. Ladies sitting side-saddle were known to abandon decorum, throw their leg astride their hunter and gallop off in pursuit of Cluricauns, much to the

chagrin of their escorts. So it was, that when the
Roscommon fairy gave chase to the risen fox, he
in turn was pursued by one of the fairest damsels
in all the baronies of Connaught. Maureen Lahy
was her name and her father was a respected
landowner in the district. This ravishing beauty
had hair as dark as a moonless night, skin as
smooth as a peach from the East and lips as red
as holly-berry. All the men of the West adored her
and sought her favours.

The Cluricaun noticed his pursuer and swerved
away from the pack, crossing a fairy rath as he did
so. Maureen followed, but when her horse came to
the rath it stopped suddenly, throwing her over its
neck. The Cluricaun returned, dismounted and
helped her to her feet. By this time the rest of the
hunt had disappeared. The stranger amazed
Maureen, because although she had never seen him
before, he asked her about her family and friends
by name. There was to be a hunt ball in Lahy's that
evening, so Maureen invited the Cluricaun to be
her guest and he gladly accepted. In return, he
urged her to enter her horse for the main event at
the Knockcroghery point-to-point race-meeting
next day. He promised to provide a jockey that
would win the race for her. Maureen smiled at this,
because her nag was as slow as a wet week. She did
as she was told, however, and next morning, when
she went to the stable to saddle up her horse, a

small man was standing in the corner all dressed up in jockey's clothes. These seemed to emit a faint amber light that had a peculiar, soothing effect on Maureen.

'I will take over now,' the small man said, hopping up on the horse's back and trotting off through the stable yard and on through the fields. Maureen joined her family in their coach and four, and soon they all reached the point-to-point venue. There was no sign of Maureen's horse and as the time approached for the race in which he was entered, she grew anxious. Ten fine beasts lined up for the start and the steward called for Little Peepers, Maureen's entry. From behind a tree-covered hillock came her horse and when the crowd saw the tiny rider they laughed loudly. Maureen's father became angry and chastised his daughter, but she told him to stay quiet and bet any money he had on Little Peepers.

'But that horse never came anywhere but last in a race,' he argued. Maureen knew this was so, and she wondered why she had given her father such foolish advice. Guided by some strange urge, Mr Lahy laid a large bet just before the race began. As soon as the flag dropped, a wind whistled loudly through the trees surrounding the field and seemed to bear Little Peepers and his rider across the highest ditches quite effortlessly. The other entries were no match for Maureen's horse and there was great jubilation as it finished three fields ahead of its rivals. Maureen ran to thank the little rider, but he had disappeared and the Cluricaun was holding the horse's halter when she arrived at the finish.

'Where is the wonderful jockey?' she asked.

'He's gone to help prepare the reception to celebrate our win. Come, I will lead you to it,' the Cluricaun answered.

Maureen had lived a sheltered life. Her mother always warned her to be wary of strange men. Now, however, accepting the invitation seemed the most natural thing in the world to do. The Cluricaun hoisted her on to his own horse, then urged it on and Maureen felt as though she were flying across a misty, light blue world of delicate flowers and gentle breezes. They came to a mansion made of a bright orange material and a dozen ladies-in-waiting danced down the steps, took her to a magnificent amethyst-tiled bathing area and gently washed her in pink water scented with aromatic oils. Then they dressed her in a magnificent ball gown of red and black and led her to the dining room. Its opulence was beyond description. Rich tapestries covered the walls and gold chandeliers hung from the ceiling. Fifty tables sagged under the weight of fine foods and wine. She ate, drank and then danced with handsome young men.

At midnight the Cluricaun asked her to dance. When he placed his right hand around her waist, she felt a peculiar burning sensation and slowly the joy she had been experiencing gave way to fear. The Cluricaun's dark eyes seemed to turn red and his nostrils flared wickedly. Among the dancers, she noticed relatives and friends of hers that had died, some many, many years before. All seemed to have vacant, expressionless eyes; all but the man with whom she danced. The music grew louder and its beat quickened. The Cluricaun whirled her around and around the floor and his hand seemed to burn her back more and more. As it did, her feet left the floor, and now they danced through a dark night sky full of bleeding stars. A purple moon shed an eerie light but it was enough for Maureen to spot her home below. This was the first time she had thought of her parents since the race-meeting and as soon as she did, she began to say a prayer for them. Only one word and one syllable of the Our Father had escaped her lips when the Cluricaun began to scream. He whipped his hand from her waist and shook and waved it about as if it was causing him great pain. He grasped it with his left hand, letting Maureen go completely. She fell, but floated downwards gently. Six rust-coloured eagles appeared, spreading their wings beneath her and conveyed her back to her own back door. Her parents welcomed her and told her she was foolish to walk home.

'You need not have been afraid of me,' said her father. 'The horse I intended to back did not win either. And sure second-last is an improvement for Little Peepers.'

Maureen Lahy kept her counsel and forgot about her adventure until the following Easter when her dressmaker was measuring her for a new gown. She remarked on the red, hand-shaped scar on Maureen's lower back.

TWO

THE MAID OF ARAN

The name Síofra means a fairy or fairy child.
Late one autumn evening, a young Aran
Island girl of that name was going to a well on
Inisheer for water. She heard a bell in her ear and
knew that this was the call of a soul in purgatory,
a plea for prayers begging its release into the
happiness of heaven. The girl murmured her Hail
Marys until her foot slipped on the wet surface
near the well and she fell. She felt that some evil

force was objecting to her prayers. When she stood up, she could not recognise the land around her. There were no familiar trees or bushes and the well had disappeared. It was night-time, yet she could observe everything. On a hill that she had never seen before, a huge fire blazed and a host of people were gathered around it. They were small, the tallest of them scarcely two feet high. As she walked towards them she could feel herself shrinking, and by the time she reached them, she too was tiny. Nobody smiled and the womenfolk cast furtive glances her way.

Suddenly the crowd parted and a handsome prince strode forward. To Síofra, it looked as if he had emerged from the flames. His long, fair hair glistened in the fire's glow and the clasp that tied it back was of gold. He wore a white cloak and fine brooches of silver and diamonds decorated his sash of crimson. To Síofra's amazement he approached her and asked her to dance. A little shy and very afraid, she muttered an excuse about there being no music. When she did, the prince waved his hand and a beam of light flashed from a huge ring on his finger. Instantly Síofra heard the most haunting music, as if it came from hundreds of stringed instruments. It was above and below her, to her left and to her right, and the prince took her in his arms and they began to dance. It was not the traditional Irish music to which Síofra normally listened, yet she was able to match her partner's every step. The others were dancing too but Síofra did not notice anybody but her prince. She gazed into his eyes and he returned her smile. They danced on and on until the moon sank behind the hill and the stars faded in the sky, yet the experience seemed to last only a few moments.

The music stopped and Síofra saw for the first time a long flight of marble steps leading down under the hill. The prince took her hand and led her to these. Everybody else followed. They arrived in a splendid banqueting hall, lit by dozens of golden sconces that seemed to emit a beautiful fragrance. Fine linen cloths covered the tables, and garlands of delicate flowers decorated them. Síofra had never seen such a sight. Liveried male servants bore silver dishes of fine food and shapely maidens in light gossamer dresses stood by, ready to serve wine into golden meidirs, the traditional regal drinking cups of Irish chieftains. As soon as they sat, the prince called for wine and offered it to Síofra. As he did, one of the male servants leaned over her and placed some veal on her plate. He also whispered in her ear: 'If you eat or drink in this place, you will never return to Inisheer again.'

She looked to see if she recognised the man, but by the time she raised her eyes, he was at the other end of the vast hall. She heeded his warning and refused the meidir that the prince still held

out to her. His countenance darkened but he
feigned a smile as he said, 'Food then? Come, you
must be hungry after so much dancing.' She
politely refused, and immediately there was a
stillness in the hall as everybody stared sullenly at
her. One swarthy, dark man approached her,
calling, 'You have come to our land and have
danced with our prince. How dare you insult us
by refusing our hospitality!'

'Disgraceful!' 'Shame!' Murmurs of disapproval
arose from the assembly and Síofra began to
tremble with fear. The dark man seized the prince's
cup and tried to force Síofra to drink from it. She
felt his rough fingers dig into her shoulder, causing
her excruciating pain and dizziness. Suddenly, the
servant who had warned her earlier appeared at her
side, seized her by the hand and led her away from
the table. The crowd jumped up, admonishing him
and uttering threats on himself and on his kinsfolk.
From beneath his waistband he took a tiny muslin
bag of eidhneán nimhe, poisoned ivy used by
ancient Egyptians for protection against evil spirits.
'Keep this in your hand until you reach home and
say your prayers somewhere else besides near the
well in future,' he advised, before leaving her at
the bottom of the marble steps.

She began to climb and the host of fairy folk
tore the sconces from the walls and sped off in
pursuit. The steps became steeper and steeper and

the walls began to close in on her. Tired and exhausted, she reached the top and had just stepped out of the hill when the gap closed behind her. She was back beside the well. From its depths she heard howling and screaming from voices raised in great anger. She filled her bucket and ran home. Her mother remarked that she was back very quickly. This puzzled Síofra. When the old lady began to poke the fire, she did not seem to hear what terrified her daughter — the voice of the dark fairy. 'The fairy folk will catch you without the sachet of ivy someday and you will not escape so easily.'

Síofra sewed the talisman into her cloak, however, and never went to the well again without it. There was one strange outcome from the episode: instead of bells in her ears thereafter, Síofra heard the music that she had danced to the night she joined in the festivities of the fairy folk. When she did, she still prayed for the souls in purgatory — as long as she was not too near the well.

THREE

THE HUNCHBACK AND THE MEAN WOMAN

Ireland's skinflints have come to realise that there is nothing the fairies dislike more than meanness, especially among folk who are not without a shilling. There lived in the hills of Donegal one time a woman who seldom gave alms. If she did, it was only what she had no use for. Foolishly, she thought that such charity would enhance her chances of salvation in the next life. Down the winding lane that led to her house came a travelling man, one day. He was a hunchback. He asked the woman's servant for the loan of a saucepan to boil himself an egg. The servant asked the woman if she could lend him one and she said, 'Of course you can.'

As the girl was taking one down from its hook, however, the woman stopped her. She said, 'Don't give him that one, you *óinseach* [foolish woman]. Hand him out the one with the hole in it and he will have to mend it before he boils his egg. That will save me paying another tinker sixpence for mending it.' The servant obeyed and, sure enough, back came the hunchback with a perfectly mended saucepan. The mean woman was delighted at her own craftiness. Only until supper-time that evening, let it be said.

The servant began to boil milk for the woman's children, who shouted at her to hurry up and pour it over their bread pieces for their nightly 'goody'. The contents of the saucepan foamed up and burnt and the smell of it wafted into the next room where the woman of the house sat eating fine food and drinking vintage wine.

'What's going on out there?' she called, dropping her knife and fork and making for the kitchen.

'The milk burnt up as fast as a match in hell, mam.'

'You useless thing! Why didn't you watch it? Such a dreadful waste of two pints of milk!' After this admonition, the mistress jumped when she heard a voice in the chimney calling, 'That will be two pence.' It was an eerie, low monotone.

The woman herself poured a quart of milk, tried to boil it, and the same thing happened.

'That pan must be dirty,' she said, examining it. 'My goodness, four pints of milk gone to waste!'

'That will be four pence,' said the voice in the chimney.

The woman made the servant scour the saucepan before trying again. Two more pints burned up and the woman was in tears at the waste. 'Six pints of milk gone on me! What will I do at all?'

This time the voice in the chimney was jeering. 'Never again try to save paying a tinker a tanner,' it echoed, and immediately a cloud of soot filled the kitchen as down tumbled the hunchback who had borrowed the saucepan. The woman and the maid screamed as the black form almost knocked them down before running out the back door, laughing loudly.

The woman became quite decent after that and as soon as she did, the saucepan never again boiled over, even when left far too long on the fire.

FOUR

THE LEPRECHAUN AND THE DANDELION

On Lady's Day, thousands of people visited Tobar Muire (Mary's Well), near Dundalk. They crept around the well on their knees, nine times in a westerly direction. This, they believed, would cure all their ills and make amends for their sins. Then they would go away and begin cutting their corn. A man called Jack Fox completed the ritual and was heading for his fine field of oats with his scythe on his back. From the hedgerow, he heard a sound like the chirp of a cricket. He wondered if it was a hoarse chaffinch, but it was not the time of the year for their song. On he walked and then he heard it again. This time it sounded more urgent. Tic-tac-too, tic-tac-too. Slowly, a possibility began to dawn on Jack and, as it did, the hair on the back of his neck stood on end.

He rose on to his toes and peeped across. Nothing. Not even the sound he had been hearing. Jack walked along further and as soon as he heard the tic-tac-too again he pulled the bushes aside and looked through. A small man sat by a last, no bigger than a farthing, shaping a tiny shoe that shone like gold. The hammer with which he worked was the size of a pin. As he tapped, a pointed cap waved backwards and forwards, almost mesmerising Jack, but not enough to divert his attention from the little shoe-maker. Jack knew he was looking at a leprechaun and he remembered hearing from his mother that the rascal could lead him to a pot of gold if he made sure to keep watching him. He laid his scythe against the hedge and crept closer.

'*Bail ó Dhía ar an obair,*' ventured Jack and quickly added, 'God bless the work,' in case the leprechaun did not know Irish.

'*Go raibh maith agat*, and thank you too,' the cobbler answered, smiling. 'It's a hot day. Maybe you'd like a drink?' He reached for a pitcher that lay beside his stool. He hoped Jack would look towards the vessel but was disappointed. Jack fixed his gaze more steadily.

'What kind of drink have you?' he asked.

'*Uisce beatha*, best of gorse whiskey.'

'There's no such thing as whiskey made from gorse. Mead, perhaps, but not whiskey.'

'Taste it then, if you don't believe me,' said the leprechaun. 'Reach down there in the hedge and fetch me a glass.' Again, Jack resisted the temptation to look elsewhere.

The leprechaun tried all sorts of ruses. He told Jack that his cattle were breaking out of the field behind him. He shouted, 'Watch out. Your scythe

is falling across your neck!' He told him he had
heather beer as well as whiskey and that if he tasted
it he would live for ever. 'The recipe is in my
family for generations. The Milesians brought it
over to Ireland and gave it to us.'

'And what might your name be?' Jack asked.

'Night and day and far away.'

'That's a funny name.'

'So is yours, Jack Fox. Do you live in a covert
up on the Cooley Mountains or what?' the
leprechaun teased.

'How do you know my name?'

'Why wouldn't I know it and I living on your
farm for years.'

Jack thought it was about time he made an
approach about the cobbler's crock of gold. 'Bring
me to the end of the rainbow where your pot of
money lies,' he ordered.

The leprechaun laughed. 'God bless us and save
us, have you heard that nonsense too?'

'Come on now. No more of your old chat.
Bring me there.' Jack grimaced as crossly as he
could and the little man began to look frightened.
Jack could see that he was still stalling, so he
issued the threat that custom demanded for such
obstinacy. 'I will bring you home and roast you
on the griddle.'

'I'll tell you where my crock of gold is, Jack, but
it's not at the end of the rainbow. Come on.' He

made to run ahead, but Jack suddenly grasped him in his hand and held him right up against his eyes for fear of being distracted. Whether he crossed a stile or climbed a bank, stumbled in rushes or leapt a stream, Jack kept his eyes glued on the back of the leprechaun's head. The fairy man led him through four small fields and into a huge, fifty acre one that was filled with dandelions. 'There you are now,' he said, pointing to one plant. 'Dig down deep under that *caisearbhán* and you will find the pot of gold. But I have to go now or the fairies will have no shoes for their big ball tonight and they will take revenge on you if that happens.'

Jack realised that he had no spade to do as he was bid. He could not even mark the spot by cutting a few dandelions near by, because he had left his scythe on the hedge where he found the leprechaun. 'Swear on your oath that the crock of gold is under that dandelion,' he ordered.

'I swear on my oath and on the oaths of all my Milesian ancestors [the last invaders of Ireland before the historical period].'

'Very well,' Jack said, 'you may go now and thanks very much. *Slán*!'

'*Slán is beannacht*, health and a blessing,' said the leprechaun, and Jack thought he noticed a glint in his eye.

Jack took off his stocking and placed it over the dandelion so that he would recognise it again.

Then he walked back to his home for a spade. He told his wife about their good fortune and said it was the luckiest Lady's Day they ever had. He promised her a new house and barn and all the finery she could ever dream of. Back he went, whistling, towards the big field. When he crossed the stile into it, he screamed in anger. Over every dandelion in the fifty acres there was a stocking the same colour as his own.

'*Ochón, ochón*, woe is me,' he wailed. 'I could be digging for the rest of my life and might not be under the right dandelion. The rogue of a leprechaun has fooled me indeed.'

A flurry of wind rose from behind him and blew across the expanse of stockings. They fluttered the exact way the leprechaun's hat had done when Jack first saw him working at his last. Jack swore he could hear the hundreds of dandelions laughing. Dejected and downcast, he returned home and told his wife his sad tale.

'Well,' she said, 'there's one consolation. I'll never have to knit you another stocking.'

FIVE

THE 'RALE OLD MOLL ANTHONY' OF KILDARE

D oes a pair of tombstones in the cemetery at
Milltown, County Kildare, conceal some
dark secret? Certainly, some people of the area are
reluctant to talk about the stones. Others will not
even tell of their whereabouts. The Death Register
kept by the Eastern Health Board dates back to
1868 — not far enough in time to clinch an
argument about one of Leinster's most famous
women, Moll Anthony.

Most practitioners in the art of curing confined
their cases to ailments of humans, but 'the rale old
Moll Anthony of the Red Hills' seems to have had
a veterinarian degree also. More, she did not always
attend at the farms of the sick beasts. Once the
animal's owner came to Moll, the beast was cured
at the moment of consultation.

Moll did not live at the Red Hills at all but
at the Hill of Grange between Milltown and
Rathangan, a likely abode, this, for a woman
regarded by some as being in league with the
fairies, because this rise, the Hill of Allen and
Donadea's Green Hill lie in a straight line. The
line was a fairy track and if a wayfarer crossed any

stile along it at the stroke of midnight, he would remain there for a month with one foot planted on either side of the stile — and in Kildare these contraptions always had a strand of barbed wire across the top. Precarious!

One of the many stories involving Moll Anthony tells how a boy once met a funeral and, as was the custom in times past, he turned to walk some of the way behind the coffin. He even helped to carry it. When the funeral came back to the lad's own gate the pallbearers left down the coffin. The boy ran in to tell his mother and when they both came back out the coffin was still there but the mourners had disappeared. They unscrewed the lid and a lovely young girl of about 12 stepped from within. She did not know who she was or from where she had come. The family adopted her and she lived happily with them, taking the mother's name, Mary. When she and the boy, James, grew up, they married.

One day, the young wife asked James to bring her with him to the fair in Castledermot. He was delighted to have her as company and so the pair set off, intent on having a good time. James had two cows to sell. They were fine animals and in no time at all a farmer from Carlow bought them and gave James a good price. As was the custom, the buyer and the seller went to a bar to drink a luck-penny cup. Mary joined them and the farmer's wife who was already waiting in the bar after her morning's shopping. When Mary entered, she stared quizzically at her. After a drink or two, the Carlow man told James that his bride was 'the spit' of his own daughter, whom he had buried many years before. The farmer's wife added, 'I thought the same as soon as I clapped eyes on her.' James asked them the date of their daughter's death. It coincided with the day he had seen the girl step from the coffin. The old farmer's wife stared at Mary again and said, 'Pull down the top of your dress, allanah.' Mary's retort stunned the other three. She said, 'It's all right, mother. The raspberry mark is still on my shoulder.'

Those who regarded Moll Anthony as being in league with the good people said she was that girl, Mary (Moll). But this type of story rightly upsets some logical thinkers. Some of them claim that Moll Anthony's father was an Anthony Dunne and that she got her name from him, because if a few families of the same name lived in an area, it was normal to append the father's Christian name to distinguish his daughter.

But what about the mysterious Milltown tombstones?

Well, Lord Walter Fitzgerald claimed that Moll Anthony's name was Leeson, that she died in 1878 and that her cure passed on to another James Leeson. This man lived in 'a comfortable slated house on the Hill of Grange' on the site of Moll's former mud-walled house. Local people accept that James had the cure and that the house that still clings to the side of Grange Hill was indeed his.

Through the ivy on one of the Milltown stones can be read the inscription:

Erected by Catherine Leeson of Grange Hill in memory of her dearly beloved husband, James Leeson, who departed this life 27 [or 22?] April 1894. Aged 64 years.

The legend on the bare stone beside it is difficult to read but it seems to be:

Erected by Mary Leeson of Punchesgrange in memory of her mother, Eliza Cronley [or Cronboy?] who departed this life 11 of Dec. 1851, aged 20 years. Also the above named Mary Leeson who died 28 Nov. 1878, aged 71 years.

Now Mary Leeson, born in 1807, could not have had a mother who died in 1851, aged 20. Eliza Cronley could possibly have been her mother if she died in 1851, aged 90, and a close study reveals that somebody could have tampered with the 9 to make a 2 in Eliza Cronley's age at death.

Was this a deliberate attempt to make the inscription appear ridiculous?

Was Sir Walter Fitzgerald right when he said
that Moll Anthony's father was Anthony Dunne?
Was it propriety that deterred him from mentioning
an unmarried mother, because a child born out of
wedlock at the turn of the nineteenth century got
little in the way of kindness — not even her own
name when grown up and decently married?

The evidence available seems to present
conclusive proof that Mary Leeson was the lady
known as Moll Anthony. Kildare folklore links her
curing powers with the fairy folk who lived in the
heart of the Hill of Allen. This was the headquarters
of the ancient Fianna; it was also the place first
visited by Oisín on his return from Tír na n-Óg.
The Hill of Allen, the Red Hills, the bleak Hill of
Grange — old people tell strange tales of the
supernatural by firesides in and around all three
areas, and in most of them, Moll Anthony figures, a
mortal among, if not definitely of, the *sidhe*.

SIX

FIONN MAC CUMHAILL AND THE SIDHE

No collection of Irish fairy tales would be complete without recalling one of the many brushes between the legendary chieftain, Fionn Mac Cumhaill, and the *sidhe*. Fionn led the Fianna, a band of warriors who acted as bodyguards to the High Kings of Ireland. Their fortress headquarters was at the Hill of Allen in County Kildare. He was far away from there one day, hunting with his hounds, Bran and Sceólan, and some of his band. They came to a hill in Breffni, which was in the Cavan region, and as they hunted, the king of the Breffni *sidhe*, Conaran, watched them from his earthen keep, Dún Conaran. Conaran envied Fionn his power and his army. At one stage in the hunt, Fionn, his hounds and his colleague Conn became separated from the rest of the Fianna. Conaran saw this as a chance to destroy Fionn.

The fairy king had three daughters. They were the ugliest and worst-tempered girls in the fairy kingdom. Their eyes were like bloodshot onions, and their noses as crooked as rams' horns. Donkeys' ears would have been prettier than theirs. Hair grew outside and inside lips that drooped to their breasts, revealing stumps of black teeth that were the shape of tombstones. It must have slipped down from their heads, because these were thatched with leeches and filthy brown reeds. When they spoke, they sounded like boars at mating time. The dreadful laughing of the Crooked Crones from Cork would have sounded like sweet music if compared with the tittering of this trio, Cuillean, Caébhóg and Iarainn. They seldom laughed, of course, and when they did, it was either at someone else's plight or to harm a human. The laugh of the *sidhe* can do untold harm.

Conaran called these daughters to look at Fionn and each one of them cackled and writhed with longing, because women of the *sidhe* are fond of human warriors. They drew their nails, that were like ravens' talons, through their leeches and studied themselves in a stream to make sure they looked all right. When they were inside the fort, you see, these girls did not realise they were ugly. And another thing, human eyes saw them as beautiful beings.

The women sat a few feet inside the entrance to the fairy fort and began spinning. Each had yarn wound around a hazel branch so that it would weave a spell. Fionn and Conn came by and noticed them. In order to get a better look, they stepped inside the boundary between their world and that of the *sidhe*. Even before they pushed the hazels aside, they were under a spell, but when they touched the wood of the branch, each of their hands felt as heavy as the Rock of Dunamase and a withering weakness trembled in their bodies. This made their necks flop about like eels, while their legs wobbled and finally collapsed beneath them.

'Your whiskers are the most beautiful things I ever saw,' Fionn said to Caébhóg. The fairy wench smiled and, luckily, Fionn closed his eyes to think, because he still realised that they were in some danger and wanted to devise some way of calling the rest of the Fianna to his assistance. If his eyes had been open, the smile would have pierced his heart.

Conn looked at Iarainn and said, 'I have travelled the length and breadth of Ireland and paid a visit or two to Alba also, but never have I seen eyes and ears as delightful as yours.' Iarainn blushed and the redness would have blinded Conn, but he too closed his eyes, the more to dwell on the apparent pulchritude of Iarainn. Before he opened them, he heard Fionn say, 'Whistle up the Fianna, Conn.' Conn vaguely remembered how he was renowned for sounding a note that carried across the western world. He smiled as he remembered how a lark from Greece once came to the Hill of Allen in answer to his whistle. So he pursed his lips to call the Fianna, but no sound came, only a kind of 'phut phut' that you would

hear when porridge was beginning to boil. He
wept, and Iarainn licked the tears from his face.
Conn thought this was the gentlest touch he had
ever experienced. Fionn looked at him, however,
and was horrified at what he saw. Conn's face was
bleeding, because the coarse hairs on Iarainn's
tongue were like briars. The three harridans then
tied up the two men with ropes of plaited bracken
and danced around them gleefully. Cuillean went
to her father and hugged him and asked him to
allow herself and her sisters to do something
terrible to Fionn and Conn. An evil grin spread
across Conaran's face, but he told his daughter to
have patience, because there were more of the
Fianna to come. Fionn Mac Cumhaill heard this.
His mighty intellect sensed further danger and he
began to resist the fairy spell. He opened one eye
slightly and noticed that the three women were not
quite as beautiful as they had first appeared. He
closed it quickly in order to concentrate more.

Meanwhile, Bran and Sceólan were barking at
the entrance to the fairy fort. Animals can always
detect the supernatural, so their baying became
louder and louder when their master did not
reappear. The remainder of the Fianna huntsmen
were chasing a magnificent black hog towards the
Leitrim border, but they heard the barking, called
off the chase and returned to Dún Conaran. There
they saw the anxiety of Bran and Sceólan at the

entrance to the fairy fort. Realising that their leader was in some danger, they rushed in, sweeping the hazel branches aside. Immediately, they suffered the same debility as Fionn and Conn. The three women tied them all up and Cuillean winked at her father and said she knew what he had meant earlier. They trussed some of the men as fowl waiting for roasting and rolled them into a dark cave, all the time screaming with glee. Others, they laid side by side and leaped up and down on their stomachs. They stood Conn on his head in a damp hole and allowed slugs and snails to crawl into his mouth, his nose and ears. Cuillean brought Fionn into a small, private cave and kissed him until his mouth festered.

When it was time to close up the fort for the night, Conaran told Caébhóg to go outside and see if she could do anything about the dogs' baying.

'We won't sleep a wink tonight after the fun,' he said, leering. As he said this, he honed his sword and Caébhóg shivered with excitement.

'Don't start any slaying until I return,' she demanded, with delight.

Caébhóg went outside. A bright moon slid from behind a rugged black cloud and she began to raise her arms to cast a dog-silencing spell on the animals. At that moment a lame man hobbled towards the fort. It was the great fighter of the Fianna, Goll Mac Morna, who had twisted his ankle and had dropped behind the others when they responded to the call of the hounds. A former leader of the Fianna, Goll was celebrated among the fairy folk as a formidable opponent. Therefore, Caébhóg decided to kill him before he entered the fort. She called in to her sisters and they came to her side. All three drew their swords and faced Goll.

'Each one of us is worth a hundred of the Fianna,' they threatened, as they called on Goll to do battle.

Goll too drew his sword and, although his ankle gave him great pain, he leaped forty feet into the air, letting out a war-cry that was heard in Wales. A man from Pembrokeshire thought it was the archangel's trumpet announcing the end of the world. Goll's foot hurt when he landed, but so did Caébhóg's head, because his heel hit her crown and drove her three feet into the boggy earth.

As always happens when the *sidhe* do battle with humans, the earth stood still, and everything on it became silent. The winds stopped blowing, the clouds ceased to move and the moon turned red. Some hounds were caught standing on their hind legs. Others balanced on three paws. Bran and Sceólan lay head to head, feet in the air. There was no more barking.

Only the combatants moved, and the swishing of their weapons made an eerie noise, the only sound heard for the next three hours of that night.

Time and time again, the women lunged at Conn but always he dodged them and slashed some part of their bodies with his sword. No matter how deeply he gashed them, there was just a small spurt of yellow blood before the wound healed. As time passed, however, his foot became swollen. It looked like a huge turnip and was the same hue. The weight of this lump made Goll tire terribly, and his battle-leaps barely brought him above the trees. He realised that he must end the fight or be slain.

Goll dropped his sword to his side. Thinking he was too tired to keep it aloft, the three women screamed with delight and formed a semicircle as they moved towards him to deliver their death thrust. When they were within six feet of him, Goll swung his sword in a mighty arc and sliced the trio in two. Three upper bodies still lashed out with swords, while three lower bodies ran around Conn, trying to trip him up. He approached the upper halves first and split each one from head to navel so that only the sword arm remained a threat. Then he kicked at the lower halves with his good foot. One of these landed in Donegal, another in Mayo and a third in west Kerry. Only the first landed on hard ground and today it is called Errigal Mountain. The others sank in marshland, and that is why people in Mayo and Kerry call this type of ground 'bottoms'.

Goll sliced off the wrist of each sword-hand then. As soon as he did, the earth trembled, the winds blew and the moon regained its former colour. The hounds leaped about and ate the bits of woman that remained scattered around. Inside Dún Conaran, the bindings fell away from Fionn and the Fianna. When Conaran saw this, he made himself disappear while the warriors uttered a great roar and dashed from the fort to clasp Goll Mac Morna in grateful embrace.

Led by their hounds, the Fianna then faced south and headed for their Hill of Allen home. They were in good spirits, singing and shouting. They were not gone a mile, however, when they heard a piercing wail and, looking behind them, they beheld a fearsome sight.

Now when Conaran the fairy king was married first, his queen lost a daughter in childbirth because she was delivered outside the fairy fort. Before they buried the infant under a thorn tree, they named her Brón, which means sorrow. It is fairy practice that an infant so deceased can re-emerge fully grown, should any human take the life of one of its siblings. Since Goll had killed three sisters, therefore, Brón returned three times the size of each sister, three times as ugly and uttering threats in a voice that was louder and more grating than anything the Fianna had ever heard before. This freak had no hair at all, but a scalp of granite. Her eyes protruded like two sheeps' bladders and her nose was the shape of the

Sugarloaf mountain in Wicklow, and not much smaller. From ears that looked like sides of beef, plants that resembled enormous nettles grew. The woman was at least twenty feet tall. Not being inside the fairy fort, her grotesqueness was evident to the Fianna.

'I demand revenge for the slaying of my sisters,' she roared, and six large oak trees fell before the thunder of her voice.

'To this you have a right,' said Fionn, calling on his son Oisín to oblige. To everybody's horror, for the likes of this never happened before, Oisín refused, saying he had lost the power of his arms. Scornfully, Fionn called on his grandson Oscar, but he too declined for a similar reason. One after another, men who were famous for their bravery refused to fight this ogress. Eventually, Goll Mac Morna spoke.

'It was I who killed this woman's sisters, so let me attempt to do battle with her.' By this time the lump on his ankle was as big as Mount Leinster and Fionn was reluctant to allow him to face such a formidable foe. Goll insisted and the fight began. The noise of battle rang throughout the land making a din that was surpassed only by Brón's terrifying shouts. Goll knew he had to win quickly, because his strength was ebbing. As in the fight with Cuillean, Caébhóg and Iarainn, he dropped his sword-arm and Brón thought he was unable to continue. She lunged forward, Goll side-stepped and slashed off her right leg. She toppled and fell against a giant oak, which collapsed under her weight. As it fell, a large branch struck her and stunned her. Goll Mac Morna moved in and cut off her head with his sword. As he held it in the air, the Fianna cheered him. Fionn complimented him and told him he would reward him with his most cherished possession.

'I have a beautiful daughter called Cebha,' he said to Goll.

'You have indeed,' said Goll.

'You may take her in marriage,' Fionn promised.

Goll thanked him. The couple married and lived happily for a while. Like many who achieve greatness, however, Goll brooded on how he saved Fionn and the Fianna and on how his own father had lost the leadership to Fionn. This injustice, as he saw it, preyed on him until he became sullen and bad-tempered. He did not know this, but the *sidhe* were putting all sorts of evil notions into his head. They arranged a quarrel between Goll and Fionn's son Cairell, getting Cairell to say 'You keep boasting about your great feat. My father would have killed Cuillean, Caébhóg and Iarainn himself but for the fact that, within the fairy fort, they looked beautifully feminine and it would have broken the rules of the Fianna to harm them.'

'Your father was afraid of them,' accused Goll.

They fought and Goll cut off his brother-in-law's head. An angry Fionn Mac Cumhaill came across his dead son. Letting out a great wail of grief, he drew his sword and slew Goll Mac Morna.

Ever after, before every hunt, he warned the Fianna not to go near a fairy fort.

SEVEN

BIDDY MANNION'S BABY

O n Inishark, off the Connemara coast, a woman called Biddy Mannion gave birth to a baby. At an early age the boy child was the spit of his handsome father and some said he was the fairest fellow ever born to a fisherman's wife. Biddy breast-fed her infant. This, the neighbours said, was beneficial to the child's health. At the same time, the king and queen of the sea fairies had a son, but the queen, God help her, was not too good at the nursing. It was not entirely her fault, because she was pining for her blackguard of a husband. Right through her confinement and after, this reprobate was away up around the Giant's Causeway having some sort of argument with another royal fairy who had come across from Scotland to cause trouble. As a result, the Scottish fairy had cursed the queen's lactation. The distraught queen employed a wet-nurse, a female seal that lived in a cave on the mainland near Cleggan. The plan was not successful. Seals are enchanted members of the Kanes who in the distant past were not too successful at breast-feeding either.

Biddy Mannion, therefore, was under observation by the special branch of the *sidhe*.

She had a protection racket going for her, however. A *bean feasa* (wise woman) gave her some charms to ward off the wee folk. These included a charred turf-sod from a Saint John's Night bonfire, which she placed under the baby's mattress. One night the child cried and Biddy took him into her own bed to feed. The little lad soon satisfied himself and fell asleep. Biddy left him in her own bed while she went to the kitchen for a cup of tea. While there, three dark men entered, took her outside, threw her across one of their horses and galloped away. There were only a few splashes as the steeds crossed the water and sped along the coast. They came to a splendid house that Biddy had never seen before. Indeed, she had never heard of anything more than a thatched cabin or two near Cleggan. A young gentleman dressed in gold and silver garments greeted her and led her indoors. He brought Biddy to a room where a young woman sat knitting. When she looked up, this stranger had a concerned expression on her face. Biddy asked why she was staring at her and the lady replied that she was recalling her own first night in the house. She had eaten and drunk to her heart's content, an unwise thing to do. It was magic fare and, by partaking of it, she became a prisoner. She advised Biddy to abstain. 'And when you get home, please ask my husband, Tim Conneely, to use his influence with the Abbot of

Cong to get me reinstated on the national census,'
she begged.

There was a knock on the door and her host
opened it. Mrs Conneely disappeared but another
worried-looking woman stood in her place. She
held a baby. The young gentleman took this and
gave it to Biddy, asking her to suckle it. She did.

Afterwards, they led Biddy to a huge dining
room. The tables were laden with the best of food
and drink. Lords and ladies sat in sartorial
splendour but they did not sneer at Biddy's worn
and faded raiment. The queen of the *sidhe* sat at
the top table and beckoned Biddy to take the seat
beside her. Poor Biddy was ravenous after her
journey, but she remembered Mrs Conneely's
warning and refused the queen's hospitality.
Instead, she requested a cure for a sick child
belonging to a neighbour on Inishark.

'Take ten green rushes from beside a well at
Aughavalla,' the queen instructed. 'Throw away
the tenth one and squeeze the sap of the other nine
into a taycup. Give this potion to the child to
drink.'

Biddy was surprised at the queen's
pronunciation, because her accent was otherwise
quite cultured. Indeed, Biddy later described the
queen as being 'like an English woman'.

Just then, the king of the fairies arrived back
from his shenanigans. The queen told him what

had happened and he gave Biddy a gold ring in appreciation. 'It will keep you from hurt and harm,' he promised. Then he rubbed ointment on her eyes and immediately she found herself in a dark, damp cave. A female seal saw her and rushed out squealing. There was a musty smell and, looking around, Biddy saw hundreds of human skeletons. The fairy king was by her side and he explained.

'These are not as they seem to you. They are the fallen angels that you mortals call fairies.' He led her to another chamber. All around it, young blindfolded children sat still upon toadstools. They did not speak and the stillness was eerie. The king whispered, 'The souls of children who died without baptism.'

'Am I in limbo, then?' Biddy asked, but received no answer. Instead, the king led her out of the cave where the sea waves rose and fell, yet were not made of water, but of grass and flowers. They walked through these. They gradually faded and withered until Biddy realised that she was back at the lane that led to her own cottage on Inishark.

'See who comes to greet you!' the fairy king exclaimed.

When Biddy looked, her escort disappeared. Who was coming down the boreen but her double. The two Biddy Mannions met and became one. Biddy raced into the house to discover her child sleeping peacefully where she had left him. Her husband came back from fishing, looked at her and shouted, 'Who the blazes gave you that expensive ring?'

EIGHT

THE HOUSE ON THE RATH

Much has been written about fairy raths and fairy paths, places where the wee folk frisk and play or have right of way. The gable wall of a Leitrim church was built on a fairy rath and the whole edifice jumped into the next field. Ill-luck befell many families who dared build on a *slígh sidhe* (fairy pass), Jim Johnson, for instance, a man from the North who settled in the West and was one sandwich short of a picnic. This was evident when he refused the warnings of neighbours about a proposed building site. They had seen the fairy host, the *slua sidhe*, dancing on a rath near Knockcroghery and would not walk across it, let alone build on it. It was there that Johnson erected a mansion of fine Wicklow granite and Cavan slate. Its interior was of carved oak and elm and a finer house was never seen west of the Boyne. Their only child, a lively 10-year-old boy wanted for nothing. He had magnificent hand-carved toys, a small pony, a donkey and a pet hen. Mrs Johnson wore gold-trimmed gowns, elegant hats and shoes, even when attending to her housekeeping. People quipped that Jim Johnson must have found the fairies' own gold in the foundations, so ostentatious was the building. Just as fine were the gardens that he set around it, all full of flowers and fruit and vegetables. The Johnsons had everything they desired, except visitors, because no neighbour would enter a house built on a fairy rath.

Jim Johnson held a house warming but nobody came to it. He, his wife and son were eating the unused food for a week and there was still plenty left when an old woman came to the door looking for a billy-can full of milk. Mrs Johnson refused. The old lady took off her blue cloak and waved it overhead as she said, 'I am asking a second and last time. Give me some milk from your fine herd, said to give the best yield in the land.' Again Mrs Johnson refused. Indeed, she called her servants and told them to chase the woman off the estate.

Next day, Jim Johnson went to the byre. His finest milch cow lay moaning and dribbling. He sent servants for a wise woman who lived in the neighbourhood and had plenty of healing mixtures. She would not come. Two days later, Mrs Johnson ordered her kitchen staff to bake bread. She left the kitchen and was knitting in the garden when the little woman in the blue cloak scurried out from behind a gooseberry bush.

'Your maids are working at the griddles,' she said. 'Please give me some fresh cake.'

'You killed our best cow. Be off with yourself,' Mrs Johnson scolded.

Again the old woman begged and again the mistress had her servant chase her away.

Over the next few days, young Johnson lost all his lively ways. He fretted about the house and turned pallid and listless. One morning he told his mother that the fairies stopped him from sleeping, that they jumped up and down on his chest until he could hardly breathe. 'They keep asking me for a billy-can of milk and a griddle cake', he said. So Mrs Johnson gave him these things to bring to his

room that night. Next morning they were gone
and the boy said that he had got a great night's
sleep. His feeling of well-being soon left him,
however, and he continued to fail. His eyes became
dull and his limbs weak and when his parents
asked him if he could explain it, he said, 'I am
exhausted from dancing with the *sidhe*. Each night
they take me through the floor, deep below the
rath on which the house stands. There I dance with
the loveliest of ladies, I eat the finest food and
drink the finest wine, but I never feel well. Please
save me, mother and father. Get a priest to bless
me or they will take me away altogether.'

Scorning both religion and the fairies, the
Johnsons were dubious, but to please their son they
sent for a priest. As soon as the holy man prayed
over the boy, he took on a pleasant countenance and
seemed tranquil within himself. He fell into a deep
sleep. Next morning his parents were full of hope
when he told them that he had not been dancing
with the fairies. They were delighted, but their joy
changed to sorrow when he continued, 'Last night I
dwelt with the angels. I roamed through a beautiful
garden where everything was calm and peaceful. The
angels told me that I would be back for good by
nightfall.' And he was. Before midnight he told his
mother that the angels were coming for him, and as
the village clock struck the hour, he passed away
peacefully, a sweet smile playing around his lips.

Jim Johnson was shattered. He neglected his farm and took to drinking heavily. His crops went unattended, his cattle remained unmilked and died bellowing. On the anniversary of his son's death, he too passed away. Full of fear, neighbours ignored Mrs Johnson, so she packed her belongings and went home to her own people in Sligo.

Lawyers put the Johnson property on the market to clear debts. A Knockcroghery man bought it, but the first thing he did after the acquisition was to pull down the house built on the rath. The land then produced the best crops in all Connaught; the cattle produced the biggest yield ever known since the legendary white cow, Bó Fin, came out of the western sea to help make Ireland a land of milk and honey; the grass grew again on the rath; and the lively music of the *sidhe* was heard from it every night of a full moon and during all the major festivals.

No woman in the vicinity ever wore a cloak of blue until ten years and a day after the demolition of the Johnson mansion.

NINE

MADGE MORAN OF MEATH

M.J. Molloy's play, *Petticoat Loose*, features fearsome fairy woman who indulged in all sorts of demonic rites. It reminded playgoers that at one time every district, barony or parish in Ireland had its own 'wise man', 'knowing woman', or 'fairy person' (the *sidhe* were early into these terms of the liberated!). According to local beliefs, these people 'had the gift', that is, they could counsel, cure or kill — well, almost. Country people feared some, dreaded a few, shunned others, but sought after most of them.

Westmeath had Conor Sheridan, the fairy doctor of Lough Bawn; Rathangan, County Kildare, had Moll Anthony; and Royal Meath had Madge Moran of Balrath.

An old woman, with hair turned back on all sides, Madge was very tiny and very neat. She dressed in a red cloak and a crisp white cap. Yet, she had an evil countenance. Her wrinkled face tapered into a pinched, pointed chin and harassed mothers threatened her on many a bold child. Madge lived in a 'bottoms', a swampy marsh near a small lake close to where Saint Scire, the great-great grandniece of Niall of the Nine Hostages, established a nunnery. Madge's most famous case concerned Terence McGrath, only son of a respectable farmer, and Alice Moore, the daughter of a small farmer. In those days 'respectable' suggested wealth rather than propriety.

Terence was a spoiled lad. His parents doted over him and gave him everything but a good trouncing that would have done him all the good in the world. He grew up a handsome man-about-Balrath, and was fond of wine, women and himself. Alas, poor young Alice Moore fell in love with him, and soon the pair were contemplating marriage. His parents did not approve of Terence's intentions and his father exhorted him to 'look a bit higher and have some of the McGrath spirit'. Perhaps Terence misunderstood his father's advice, but in any case after a few secret meetings with Alice the poor girl became pregnant. The rogue kept away then all right and his delighted parents covered up for him. They spread a rumour that their son was about to marry a 'girl of his own station' whose father had more than a few acres of prime fattening land on Boyneside.

Meanwhile the distracted Alice went to consult Madge Moran who seemed to relish the assignment, remarking, 'McGrath was always a jackeen since a yard made him a coat.' She had disliked the youth since the day he accused her of having truck with the good people. Poor Alice had

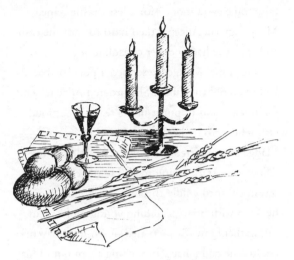

only a half a crown to offer Madge and the old
woman scraped at her pipe a while before
consenting to help. 'I'll do it but don't ever tell the
mother that bore you or the priest that christened
you.' Then she told Alice to come the following
night and to bring three flannel sheets, three
candles, a sheaf of clean corn and some
refreshments. They would need the refreshments
because they would be working all night, Madge
explained. When questioned about the work, she
shrieked in delight and described how, from the
stroke of midnight, they would be digging a grave
for a young man.

A bright young girl was Alice. She immediately
saw the sinister implications and refused to be a
party to them. She offered to wait until she could

raise some extra money for a less drastic remedy. Madge agreed. Alice worked hard to earn the cash and then she had another consultation.

This time, Madge prescribed a powder that she had in an old snuff-box. She ordered Alice to send for Terence and to put it in his tea. Alice, proud girl, refused to invite the scoundrel to tea, so Madge administered the powder herself and the fellow went stark raving mad. He roared and screamed, sped wildly through the woods, tearing his flesh with briars, catching young rabbits and eating them raw. Farmers tied down their haycocks because he had a habit of kicking them out of his way. Schoolchildren ran home when they saw him, because one day he caught a little boy by the arm and flung him into the middle of the next parish.

Horrified, Mr and Mrs McGrath engaged all sorts of doctors and specialists. Each and every one of them was perplexed, and Terence remained a maniac for four months. One day he was swinging from a tree branch near Alice's house, when he heard a scream from within. He dashed over and, looking across the half-door, perceived the midwife about her business with poor Alice on the settle. So perturbed was he by Alice's agony that he called out, 'Oh, please marry me, Alice.'

Without knowing it, he was now halfway towards breaking Madge Moran's spell. If Alice accepted, his madness would leave him and all would be well. (Perhaps it was at such junctures that fairy serials broke for commercials!) Could a girl in Alice's condition consent? Made pregnant by a man who ran away, who developed a great madness and was even now frothing at the mouth like a hungry ass as he leaned across the half-door! And asking her to marry him!

Just then the baby was born and Alice, realising that Terence was, after all, the father, consented. As soon as she did, Terence became his old self again. More — he developed a bit of backbone and went up to his parents, boldly proclaiming that he was about to marry Alice.

This he did. Some people even say that Madge Moran was matron-of-honour at the wedding!

TEN

THE RATHCOFFEY POOKA

F airy lore in some parts of Ireland projected the pooka as a phantom goat that contaminated wells and crops. In most areas it was a giant black horse that often galloped on cloven hooves like the devil. Within the fine mansion of Hamilton Rowan in Rathcoffey, County Kildare, however, the pooka appeared as a big donkey.

It was during the Rising of 1798 and the great landowner was abroad. The servants still cooked for themselves and for the farm hands, so there was always plenty of crockery for washing up after meals. In the master's absence, when the last meal of the day was over, the household left the dirty dishes in the scullery until the following morning. They sat around the fire in the huge kitchen and amused themselves telling ghost stories. This was mock bravery, because nobody ever referred to something that caused great worry each night: the banging and clattering of kitchen utensils, pokers, tongs and bellows, all accompanied by loud laughter. There was a good side to it, because each morning the delf stood gleaming on the shelves, the fire was blazing merrily in the hearth and the kitchen and scullery were spotless. Each servant hoped some of the others had risen early to tidy up, but was afraid to enquire. There could have been a more sinister explanation.

One night, the story-telling took longer than usual. A scullery boy could not get near the fire, and he did not understand some of the yarns being spun. Somewhat bored, he crept under the settle bed, covered himself with a rug and fell asleep. Nobody noticed this, and when the last servant raked the fire with ashes, put out the lamp and went to bed, the lad continued sleeping. Awakened by the sound of the back door opening, he pulled down the rug and peeped out. A big donkey was closing the door with a flick of his tail. The boy rubbed his eyes to make sure he was not dreaming, but the animal sauntered over to the fire and sat on his haunches. It looked into the ashes for a while, then yawned and spoke in a peculiar bray. 'I suppose I might as well begin.'

The terrified boy thought the donkey was going to begin eating him, but instead, it took the poker and stirred up the fire. Then it placed some turf on it and settled a cauldron on the hook. It fetched the water bucket, which was empty. 'Humph!' it grunted, then went to the well and filled it. While it was away, the boy got himself into a corner where he could see more without being discovered.

The donkey returned, filled the cauldron and sat with its back to the boy, waiting for it to boil. The animal began to sing but stopped suddenly after one verse and shouted, 'I suppose you think I can't see you, young fellow.' With that, it swung around and grabbed the boy. It held him over the cauldron and the wee fellow screamed with fear. Then the pooka flung him back in under the settle where the poor lad's teeth chattered with fright. It kept guffawing and, in a dance-like motion, went about the kitchen dusting shelves, washing the table and sweeping the floor. The water in the cauldron bubbled, so the pooka took it to the scullery and the boy heard it laughing more as it washed and dried all the crockery and put each item in its proper place. The lad wondered how an ass could know so much. When everything was tidy, the pooka raked the fire again and took one last look around. 'They will think you a great scullery lad,' it brayed, and laughed its way out into the night.

Next morning, the boy told his story. Some of the maids believed him; others did not. A clever lass from Staplestown suggested that they should do no more washing or ironing or cleaning, but leave everything for the pooka to look after. All agreed, and all day they had a great time lazing about and telling stories.

That night, the scullery boy made sure to be in bed early. The other servants stayed a while chatting, but before midnight all retired for the night and slept. Next morning, each one approached the kitchen full of anticipation. The plan had worked: the housework had been attended to and everything was spotless.

As time passed by, the household got lazier and lazier. Some servants took to drinking and the farm hands complained that, while the kitchen was spotless, the staff were neglecting their cooking duties. They heard the stories about the pooka and wished they could persuade it to take on outdoor chores. With this in mind, a ploughman sneaked into the kitchen one night when the servants had gone to bed. The pooka arrived and the ploughman spoke up.

'You are making the servants here lazy, sir. Why do you not come in daylight for a change and maybe do a bit of ploughing or harrowing or pulping mangolds?'

'My good man,' said the pooka, 'I must do all my work in the kitchen and scullery.'

'And why, pray?' the ploughman asked.

'Sit down there and I'll tell you,' said the ass.

They sat. The ploughman offered the pooka a drag of his pipe and thought he noticed the animal flinch as it refused. It began nervously.

'When Master Hamilton Rowan was an infant, I was a servant here. Although a lazy human, I received kind treatment from your master's father. He gave me shelter, clothing, food, even a few drinks, but I was the world's worst idler. A sick sparrow would do more in a week than I did in my lifetime. So, when I died and faced the Eternal Judge, he chastised me and said that before saving my immortal soul, I would have to become an enchanted animal attending to the *sidhe*, a pooka. To add to my shame, I would appear in the form of that most derided beast, the donkey. I would take on all the chores that I had neglected while alive. I would have to be cheerful about it too. This completed, I would have to go back out into the night and stand frozen in a wet fairy rath until morning, when the wee folk would find something else for me to do. So you see, my good man, I cannot perform your tasks for you, but must slave away here each night and laugh at my own misery.'

The ploughman was sorry for himself, because he could not get the pooka to perform his duties. But he was sorry for the animal too. So too was one of the servants. On being awakened by the commotion, she had crept downstairs and overheard the conversation. She came into the kitchen, carrying her best red wool coat. 'You have been very good to us, sir,' she said. 'Take this coat and keep yourself warm.'

The girl and the ploughman helped the animal into the coat. They stuck the two forelegs in each arm and buttoned the garment across the creature as if it were human.

'Give me a mirror until I see myself,' said the ass. They did this and the pooka laughed louder than ever and thanked the donor profusely. With its dance-like steps, it waltzed around the kitchen floor, then lifted the latch and slid out into the night.

'Wait! Wait!' shouted the servant. 'What about the washing and cleaning? You haven't attended to that!'

'And I won't any more,' brayed the pooka, 'because now I am free. My punishment was to last until somebody appreciated my labours enough to give me a reward. You have done this and I thank you. But now I am released from my obligation, from the fairies and from my pledge. My soul is saved and I will depart this earth for ever.' So saying, the pooka galloped into the night. As it passed the Green Hill near Donadea, it let a last long laugh and a wise woman who lived there stirred in her bed, nudged her husband and said, 'He who laughs best laughs last.'

From that day to this, nobody ever showed proper appreciation of the great things achieved by Kildare men.

ELEVEN

THE CHURCHYARD BRIDE

The Leannán Sidhe was a fairy lover, normally female, who inspired poets in return for their love. Occasionally it was male and sometimes it could adopt either form. When such was the case, it struck particular terror into the hearts of country people, because a bisexual fairy could be the Devil himself.

A tiny churchyard in Erigle Truagh, in the barony of Truagh, County Monaghan, was unique in that it had its own Leannán Sidhe. This fairy watched over corpses buried in the stony earth, but often left its post to tempt poetic relatives of the dead. At funerals it took particular note of the person who was last to leave the graveside, normally the person who composed the epitaph of the deceased. That person was almost certainly paid a visit during the following weeks — if something more dreadful did not occur.

You see, the Leannán Sidhe could actually approach the mourner on the spot. If it was a male, the Leannán Sidhe took on the form of a beautiful young woman who inspired the swain with a charmed passion, kissed him and promised to meet him a month from that day, when he would compose brilliant verse.

The trouble was, however, that as soon as the young besotted fellow left the churchyard, he remembered the local tradition and became deeply depressed, because tradition declared that the man so kissed would be buried in the same cemetery on the same day of the following month. Similarly, if the tarrying mourner was a poetess, a fairy in male form seduced her.

One such victim had just been married and was madly loved by her handsome young husband. He composed a song called 'The Churchyard Bride' after the lovely young Aileen O'More fell victim to the Spectre of Death, the Fairy of Erigle Truagh,

the Leannán Sidhe. Fittingly, the sad story is
recorded in verse, often sung to the air of 'The
Dawning of the Day'.

> The night was calm, and a clear full moon
> Was beaming o'er hill and lea,
> As I parted my true-love all too soon,
> Beneath the trysting tree.
> My thoughts flowed on to the morrow's noon —
> To the hour so long deferred;
> When away down the vale rose a doleful wail,
> And this is what I heard:
> Aileen O'More! Aileen asthore!
> From thine earthly bondage come;
> Aileen O'More! on the fairy shore
> Thy kindred call thee home.
>
> I hastened back to the myrtle bower,
> I found my darling there,
> Her form bent low like a faded flower,
> The death dew on her hair.
> I clasped her hand — Ah, why did I cower!
> No pulse within it stirred.
> Whilst once again that dolorous strain
> In the haunted vale I heard:
> Aileen O'More! Aileen asthore!
> From thine earthly bondage come;
> Aileen O'More! on the fairy shore
> Thy kindred call thee home.

In a lonely nook we laid her at rest,
And we decked her grave with flowers;
But their bloom was crushed by my heaving
    breast
Through all the weary hours —
Till the midnight came, when a phantom guest
Stood nigh where my love was interred;
As she stole away in the dawn of day
This warning voice I heard:
Phelim, asthore! Weep no more,
For soon the time will come,
When, thy bondage o'er to the spirit-shore,
Thy bride will bear thee home!

TWELVE

THE MAGIC LAPWING

The lapwing, known in Ireland as the *pilibín*, is white with black and green upper parts. It is also called a pee-wit, after its excited call that rises on the second syllable. An Pilibín Glas Bán (the Green-white Lapwing) was one such specimen. This bird conveyed messages from the fairies of the West of Ireland to certain mortals. It was particularly attentive to people of royal blood.

Once upon a time, an eagle led the birds of the air in a fight against the rodents of Clare. A prince supported the animals. The birds won and the prince, in a fit of rage, fired his gun and wounded the eagle. He brought the bird home and locked it in a royal stable for a year and a day, giving it nothing but water and an occasional fistful of oats. When he finally released the bird, it flew away, shouting as it did: 'You treated me badly for a year and a day. I now curse you to a life of wandering. You will never sleep two nights in the same bed or eat two meals at the same table until you find An Pilibín Glas Bán.'

The prince was due to marry the lovely daughter of a wealthy merchant, so he asked his father's advice. The king said he had no option but to obey An Pilibín Glas Bán. He then gave his son two cakes of soda bread, his best steed and sent him away in search of the fairy bird.

The prince rode well and covered many miles before darkness fell. He tethered his horse and lay down under a large oak tree, covering himself with moss and twigs. Before he could get to sleep, a small weedy man came along and called, 'Welcome to the son of the King of Ireland!' The prince thanked him for his welcome but asked how the man knew who he was. He replied, 'Never mind how I know your name or what you seek. I cannot tell you the whereabouts of An Pilibín Glas Bán tonight, but keep riding and tomorrow night I may have some information.' This little man was a Fear Gurtha. Such a fairy sometimes casts hungry grass (*féar gurtha*, not to be confused with the thrower) beneath the feet of travellers, causing them to waste away from hunger. At other times, he tests the charity of mortals. This one was a guide from the *sidhe*.

The Fear Gurtha was true to his word, and as the prince began eating his first soda cake the next evening, the little man appeared again and asked the prince for the crumbs that fell on the earth. The prince offered him a good thick slice of the bread and the Fear Gurtha ate it ravenously. Then he told the prince that if he rode a little more, he would pass the wood where An Pilibín Glas Bán

lived. The prince was pleased to learn that a
beautiful young woman would meet him.

'Her name is Sarah. When she looks at you,
you stare at her. When she laughs at you, you
laugh at her. When she tells you to come in with
your horse, do so,' the Fear Gurtha instructed.
The prince did as he was told. He met the girl,
who beguiled him with her beauty. Her hair was
black and shiny like the ebony in the fireplace at
his father's palace. Large green eyes smiled from
beneath finely shaped brows and a strange misty
aura enveloped her face. Sarah invited him into the
wood and led his horse to a stable that stood beside
a large purple house. Then she told him that An
Pilibín Glas Bán was awaiting him inside.

Delighted at completing his quest so soon, the
prince's joy changed to shock when he entered.
The small lapwing revealed to him that he was the
bird that he had kept locked up and starving.

'But I shot at an eagle,' the prince protested.

'You shot me. I am the messenger of the *sidhe*
and I can take on many forms,' the *pilibín* lilted
excitedly. 'And I now command you to perform
three tasks. If you fail, I will behead you and send
your head back to your father on this.' An Pilibín
Glas Bán seized a long sword from the wall and
brandished it wildly before disappearing.

Sarah returned then and led the prince to a
bedroom where he had a pleasant night's sleep.

Next morning, she prepared breakfast, but as soon as he dipped his spoon in the egg, An Pilibín Glas Bán fluttered down from the thatch and ordered him to work.

'Out you go to that hay shed, and we'll see how you like a little ill-treatment, Prince. Take this grape [fork] and move out all the straw, surely fifty tons of it, until you find the needle my granny lost there last century. That should settle your hash for you.'

The prince went to work, but for every forkful he tossed out of the shed, two came back in. For every two he threw out, four came in; for every four, eight; and so on. Desperate, and fearing he would lose his life, the prince worked until the perspiration ran from his body and formed a stream outside the door. He cried too and the stream became a torrent. From the swirling water stepped Sarah, who told him that An Pilibín Glas Bán would be out of the way for a while, reading a little and having a short nap. 'Give me the fork,' she commanded. The prince did do. She had the hay cleared in no time and there, beneath, was the needle. She picked it up and stuck it in the prince's lapel, telling him to give it to An Pilibín Glas Bán.

When the bird came along later to inspect the work and, no doubt, to have a good laugh at his former captor's predicament, the prince gave him the needle. He became greener with temper. 'Very good. You are the first man ever to have completed the first task,' he said. Behind the praise was the suspicion that his fairy daughter had worked magic on the prince's behalf.

'Your second task will begin at dawn tomorrow. You will plough and harrow the *bánóg*. It is small — only a couple of acres — but it is my favourite green patch, so do it well. Have a good sleep.' The prince detected a sneer on his captor's bill. He rose and went to work at dawn. As soon as he left the house, An Pilibín Glas Bán locked up Sarah in the harness room.

The prince's share had hardly sunk into the sod when it hit a rock and broke. He was afraid to go back and look for another plough, so he sat by the fence and wept. After lunch, An Pilibín Glas Bán again read and took a nap. Sarah called a servant and asked for a drink of water. As soon as she got it, she turned herself into a tadpole, spilled the water on the ground and swam out under the harness room door to a stream that flowed past the *bánóg*. There she changed herself back into human form.

'You're not doing too well,' she smiled.

'Indeed and I'm not,' answered the prince.

'Here, give me the reins.' Sarah urged the horses on and, even with the broken share, she turned the straightest furrow the prince had ever seen. In less time than it takes to tell, she ploughed and harrowed the field. Then she told the prince to bring the animals back to the stable yard. He did so and An Pilibín Glas Bán emerged, fresh after his rest. When the prince told him that the work was completed, he did not believe him. But he flew up into the air and saw for himself. As he re-alighted he gave the prince his third and hardest task.

'You see that castle on the hill that rises above the wood?' he asked.

'I do,' answered the prince.

'There is a hen in its highest turret who has sat on a clutch of eggs for four hundred years. Tomorrow you must go there and fetch me both the hen and the nest of eggs. If you don't, or if you break even one egg, I will behead you with this sword,' he said, brandishing the weapon again.

Next morning the prince set off. He reached the building and examined it. It had no door, window or outer stairs. How was he to get to its highest turret?

Back, locked in the harness room, Sarah again anticipated An Pilibín Glas Bán's rest period. She worked the same ruse to get out and soon joined the prince at the castle. She gave him a magic wand and told him to touch her with it and then kill her. 'Cut me in two. Place one set of my ribs against the wall and they will form stairs halfway up. Then attach the other set of ribs and you will have steps to the top.'

The prince cried more and protested. 'You have been so good and kind and helpful. I cannot kill you.'

'If you don't, the two of us will be slain,' she said. 'Do as I say, and when you are coming down the steps with the hen and the eggs, touch each step with the wand and by the time you reach the bottom, I will be restored.'

The prince did as she had instructed. Sarah's mutilated sides brought him to the high turret where he grabbed the hen and the eggs and ran back to descend. But when the hen saw bright daylight after being so long indoors, it pecked the prince's hand, making him forget to tip the first couple of steps with the wand. When he remembered and struck the fourth step, he, the hen and the nest came tumbling down and Sarah stood before him. Unfortunately, she was tilted to one side, being short three ribs. Under her instructions, the prince again returned to the green house and again An Pilibín Glas Bán emerged after his rest. When he saw the hen and the eggs he was dumbfounded.

'You surely are the best man that ever came this way,' he smiled. 'You must marry my daughter, Sarah. I will give you the castle and all the wealth you could wish for.'

That was the first time the prince realised that Sarah was the bird's daughter. It was also the first time he did not detect malice in the voice of his captor.

'I would love to marry Sarah, sir, but first I must go back and tell my parents.'

'Go then, but make a solemn promise that you will return.' There was affection in the voice of An Pilibín Glas Bán.

That night there was feasting and dancing and when the revelry ended, the prince held Sarah in his arms and kissed her. She warned him that he was never to kiss another until he returned. 'If you do, you will forget all about me,' she said.

Next morning, the prince mounted his steed and returned to Ireland. His mother saw him reining in and ran out to kiss him. The poor woman was deeply hurt when he refused. So too were his relatives and friends, none of whom he dared even embrace. His pet dog, however, jumped up on his chest and nuzzled his damp mouth against the prince's. As soon as he did, the prince forgot all about An Pilibín Glas Bán, the tasks and the help he had received from Sarah. He lived happily with his parents for a few weeks, until the King of Ireland reminded him of the rich girl he had been courting before he left.

'Left where? I never left this place.' The king did not like the strange look in his son's eyes as he uttered those words. But he held his counsel. He arranged a banquet, intending to announce that the wedding would take place the following day.

Far away, in the purple house in the wood at the end of the world, Sarah sensed that something was wrong. She seized the hen that had been hatching for four hundred years and a lazy cock that was around the farmyard as long as she could remember. Mounting her father's finest mare, she galloped towards Ireland. She landed near Wexford and asked for lodgings. When he heard how far she had come, her kindly host threw a party. Sarah remained aloof, but after midnight she asked for a few oats for her fowl. She scattered these on the floor and the cock and hen started picking at them. Suddenly, the cock pecked the hen's neck.

'Why did you do that?' the hen scolded. 'Do you not recall when I tossed out the hay and found my great-grandmother's needle for you?'

They ate more oats and again the cock pecked the hen on the neck.

'Why did you do that?' the hen scolded. 'Do you not recall when I ploughed and harrowed the *bánóg* for you?'

Again the fowl ate and again the cock pecked the hen's neck. Once more the hen chided.

'Why did you do that? Do you not recall when I killed myself getting the hen and eggs from my father's castle for you?'

At that moment the prince realised that he wanted to marry somebody more precious than the rich girl of his father's choice. He also remembered everything that the dog's kiss had obliterated from his mind: An Pilibín Glas Bán, his difficult tasks and the lovely Sarah. At that moment, too, the

King of Ireland wondered why he had thrown a party for a strange girl. He was confused when he thought he saw a hen and a cock on the dance floor one moment, the cock biting the hen's neck, and they both disappearing the next.

To his son the prince, however, everything was clear. He looked around and saw Sarah smiling at him. A few oats trickled from her hand and the prince moved closer and gave her a gentle love bite on her fair neck.

The prince and Sarah married next day and the couple lived happily ever after.

THIRTEEN

THE FEAR DEARG AND THE PRINCESS

'There's a stepmother's bite in that day.' The Irish saying is as unkind to stepmothers as is its fairy lore. These women are always depicted as being cruel to the children they did not bear. One such person, a Carlow woman, had a daughter of her own when she became widowed and then married the King of Leinster. The girl's name was Gunóg. The king too had a daughter who bore no other name but Beanflaith, meaning princess. This girl was very beautiful and the stepmother became extremely jealous of her. She decided to send her

on a hazardous errand and consulted a blind saoi, or wise man, who lived near the palace. On his advice, she dispatched Beanflaith to the Eastern World to find and bring back three bottles of healing water, *uisce sláinte*. She gave Beanflaith a small amount of food for her journey.

The girl had barely begun her journey when she met a Wicklow Fear Dearg. This is a small fairy who wears a red cap and cloak and can steal a baby from a crib and leave a changeling from his own people in its place. He can do good too, if treated kindly.

'Give me one of your juicy crubeens, gentle lady,' he asked.

'God knows, I don't have much, but what I have I will share with you, my wee man,' Beanflaith answered with a smile. They ate heartily and Beanflaith then stood to continue her journey. Before leaving, she told the Fear Dearg of her quest.

'Sit down out of that and listen to my advice,' ordered the fairy. Beanflaith obeyed and the man told her how her stepmother was acting out of ill-will. He also told her how to accomplish the task without being harmed. 'Just do whatever you are told by whomsoever you shall meet and you will be all right. Now, away with you *agus go n-éiri an bóthar leat*' (and may the road rise with you, i.e. safe journey).

When she reached the well and leaned over its parapet to fill the first bottle, a mighty dark man

arose from beneath the water. 'Wash me and clean
me and leave me back in the water,' he
commanded. Although taken aback, Beanflaith
remembered the Fear Dearg's advice and obeyed.
A second dark man then arose and asked the same.
She washed and cleaned him and left him back
too. When she did the same with the third and
fourth dark men, the bottom of the well turned
to blood and the top, honey. Beanflaith filled her
bottles and as she did, the four men came out of
the water again. They conversed about how to
reward her and one made her even more beautiful
than before. The second gave her protection against
her enemies. The third told her that everything she
touched thereafter would taste like honey. 'And
what will you give this lovely girl as a present?'
they asked the fourth. 'I will give her this. She will
have something more every evening than she
started the day with and will have eternal
happiness.'

Beanflaith returned home and handed the
bottles to her stepmother. When she saw the girl's
increased beauty and happy smile and when
Beanflaith told her what happened, the woman was
furious. Off to the saoi she went and gave him a
tongue-lashing. 'Instead of bringing her harm, you
brought her good fortune,' she chastised. The old
man advised her then to send her own daughter,
Gunóg, on the same errand. 'Then she will be the

loveliest and luckiest woman in the world,' he
said.

She sent Gunóg off and she too met the Fear
Dearg. He asked for a crubeen but she refused,
saying, 'Away out of that, you wizened and warty
creature. How dare you approach a well-bred lady
like me!'

She reached the well in the Eastern World and
the first black man popped up and asked her to
wash him and clean him.

'Me, a fine lady, wash the likes of you?' she
screamed in dismay. 'I will do no such thing.'

She told the same thing to the second, third
and fourth. When she uttered her last refusal, the
bottom of the well turned to honey and the top
turned to blood. Gunóg filled her bottles and left
for Ireland, not knowing that the four dark men
had arisen from the well and were casting curses on
her. When her stepmother saw her, she nearly
fainted. Gunóg was uglier than before and she
wore a black scowl and talked in a cantankerous
manner. There was a horrible smell from her and
anything she touched turned filthy. That night, the
old *saoi* got the length and breadth of the
stepmother's tongue. 'The girl is like a gaol door
with the bolt pulled — useless!' she said.

During the following months, the stepmother
grew more and more angry, while her daughter
grew crosser and crosser. Everything she touched

turned to powder and the king wondered why his palace was falling asunder.

Consumed with jealousy, the stepmother eventually put Beanflaith in a barrel, got her own family to help her roll it to Wexford and throw it over a cliff into the sea. Huge waves buffeted the barrel and Beanflaith was feeling sick when, all of a sudden, she felt herself rolling gently along some very soft surface. She pushed for all she was worth, prised the barrel open and gasped at what she saw. A bright sun shone down from a cloudless sky on lush green fields whose hedgerows sparkled with flowers of diamond and silver. A handsome young man with fair hair and blue eyes was smiling at her.

'I saw the barrel heading for the rocks and waded out to bring it here,' he said. The couple went to the young man's house and the family welcomed Beanflaith and invited her to stay with them. She did, and the couple fell in love and married. One year later, Beanflaith gave birth to a child.

She felt a little lonely for her own people, however, so she wrote to her stepmother asking for news of her father and members of the household. The stepmother told nobody of this, but took a magic wand given to her by the *sidhe* and set out to visit Beanflaith. Gunóg came too. When they landed, Beanflaith rushed to meet them, but instead of a kiss, the stepmother slapped her across

the face with her wand, uttered a curse and
Beanflaith was turned into a hare. She struck
Gunóg with the wand too and, although it did not
improve her appearance, the spell made Beanflaith's
husband think Gunóg was his wife. The
stepmother knew that Beanflaith, although now a
hare, could converse with her husband after dark,
so each night she gave the young man a potion
that made him sleep through until dawn.
Beanflaith came to his bedroom window each
night and told her woeful tale, but he could not
hear her.

Realising that she could not stay on the island
for ever, the stepmother asked the young man to
hunt a hare for her, saying Gunóg had creeping
sciatica and needed soup made from a hare from a
magic island to cure it. Neither the young man nor
his family had ever heard of such a thing as a hare,
let alone seen one, but the wicked woman
described the animal to them and assured them
that there was such a beast on the island.

So the young man set off to hunt the hare, not
knowing that if he killed it, his lovely wife would
be lost for ever. When Beanflaith saw him, she
longed to run up and kiss him, but the protection
given to her by the dark man of the well urged her
on. The hunt continued for three days, and as the
young man returned to his home on the third
evening, who should he meet but the Fear Dearg

that had advised Beanflaith in the first place. This little man told the young man all about Beanflaith's stepmother and her evil intentions. He said, 'The hare you hunt is your wife. The unfortunate girl comes to your window every night but cannot talk to you because you are in a deep sleep. Tonight, find some way to avoid drinking the potion.'

When he reached home and announced that he had not killed the hare, the stepmother said, 'Tomorrow you will. Get to bed early and have a good sleep.' But when she handed him the potion he pointed to the roof and said, 'Isn't that a beautiful bird that has started building in the thatch?' The woman looked up and as she did, the young man spilled the drink on to the fire. There was a loud explosion and a purple flame leaped up the chimney. When the woman recovered her composure, the young man was rubbing his lips, saying, 'That is truly the nicest drink I ever had.' He rubbed his eyes and went to bed, feigning heavy snoring within minutes. When the stepmother heard this, she smiled and went to her own bed, contented.

Beanflaith, still a hare, came to the bedroom and spoke words of love to her husband. He promised to release her from the spell the next day. At dawn, he arose and crept into the room where Gunóg and her mother slept. He took the woman's magic wand from under the bed and touched her and her daughter with it. Both of them turned into rock and rolled from the bed, out the door and into the field behind the house. But for the spell of protection from the first dark man of the well, the stones would have crushed Beanflaith, now returned to her human state and running to fall into the arms of her beloved husband.

FOURTEEN

THE SEVEN YEAR SON

A County Clare farmer's daughter became
pregnant by the son of a king of Thomond.
His queen was in league with the fairies, who
advised her to pick certain herbs and hang them
from the ceiling in her kitchen. They said that no
child would be born to the farmer's daughter while
they hung there. The farmer did not know about
this and he wondered why his daughter had
morning sickness every day for seven years. He was
destitute from paying priests, doctors and all sorts
of quacks and faith healers. Some of them told the
farmer his daughter was pregnant, but he would
not believe them, naturally, because no
confinement ever lasted that long.

A traveller called at the farmer's house one day.
He had not called there for some years and so he
noticed the decline in the property. 'What
happened to make you so down and out?' he
asked. The farmer told him the whole story and
the traveller offered to have a look at the girl. He
too confirmed the girl's condition but he told the
farmer he would try to help. Off he went to the
royal kitchen, hoping to sell some goods to the
king's household. He took out besoms and sleans

for display and while the staff examined these he
looked around and saw the herb-bag, now dirty
and black, hanging from the rafters. As he gathered
up his things, he deliberately swung the slean high
and cut it down. At that very moment the farmer's
daughter gave birth to a boy. Because of his
delayed arrival, they called him Seven Year Son.

He grew into a strong lad, because the *sidhe* had
nourished him while in his mother's womb. At 15
years of age he stopped the king's coach and four in
full gallop by hanging out of it. Then he jumped in
and asked the king for his daughter's hand in
marriage. The king told him he would have to
undergo some tests to prove himself worthy.

The first was to go over to England and make
his brother, the King of England, laugh three
times. Each chuckle would have to be loud enough
to be heard in Clare. Seven Year Son crossed the
sea and met the king, but it is hard to amuse
English royalty. Even though he drank with him all
night and told every story he could muster, there
was no laugh out of the monarch. Next day the
king told him to look after his cattle and to follow
them as far as they went grazing. They came to a
patch of hungry grass, a fairy trap for mortals.
Seven Year Son stepped on it and a large wall
appeared before him. He battered his head against
it and made an entrance for the cattle. Inside was
an orchard where an abundance of huge red apples

hung from the trees. The trees were high, so the lad climbed one and began eating the fruit.

A giant came along and picked up one of the cows and stuck it under his arm. He was walking away with it when Seven Year Son called after him, saying it belonged to the king. The giant was furious, so he flung the beast into the tree. The Irish king's son caught it by a horn and climbed down the tree with it. He left it with the others and although only up to his knees, he began wrestling with the giant. In no time at all he had the giant screaming for mercy. In return for mercy, he offered the lad a lamp that would light the world. Seven Year Son took it, then made a swipe at the giant's poll with it. The blow took the head clean off at the neck. It went bouncing around the orchard and the lad chased and kicked it. The head kept abusing the lad, when who should come by but the King of England and he let out a laugh that was clearly heard in Clare.

The king was even happier next morning when his herd yielded more milk than the palace had vessels to hold. He sent Seven Year Son off with the cows again and the same thing happened when they came to the hungry grass. When the boy was gorging himself in the tree, a double-headed giant loomed up. They threw insults at each other and again this led to wrestling and the giant's pleas for mercy. He said, 'I will give you the Sword of

Strength if you release me. You are the strongest man I ever met, but this will make you the divil entirely.' The lad took the sword and sliced the two heads off the giant with it. They hopped around the trees and the boy chased them shouting that this was the best game of football he ever had. The heads kept hurling abuse and the King of England passed by and laughed louder than before. This time, people in Aran as well as Clare heard it.

When the King of Ireland heard the guffaw, he was amazed. A little worried too, and wondering what a wedding would cost him, because the farmer's son was now two-thirds of the way towards winning his daughter's hand. Things were becoming even more complicated because, unknown to her father, the King of England's daughter had her eye on Seven Year Son. His feats of strength and good looks impressed her.

Next day, the lad set off again with the king's cattle. Things happened as before, only this time the giant that appeared had three heads. He really abused Seven Year Son. 'You're nothing but a low-down Irish coward. You picked on my young brothers yesterday and the day before. They were only 100 and 200 years old — scarcely out of the crib.'

'About time they thought of getting out of the envelope,' quipped the Irish lad, jumping down and beginning to wrestle.

This time, when the giant was appealing for mercy, he offered Seven Year Son the keys of a silver castle that suddenly appeared, as castles tend to do in fairy stories. 'Inside there is all the wealth you could wish for and, what's more, I will become your butler,' he promised.

Seven Year Son took the keys but scolded, 'If I need a butler, he won't be an ugly-looking gazebo with three heads and not a whit of manners in him.' With that, he drew the Sword of Strength and chopped the three heads off as if they were ears of corn. He began playing football with them, dribbling and hopping one against the other. When he kicked the three of them in the air at once, the King of England arrived and let out the most enormous laugh ever heard in that country before or since. The King of Ireland heard it and realised that he should send out the wedding invitations.

Seven Year Son knew he had completed his work, but he decided to have a look about the silver castle before he returned to Ireland. In its kitchen an old man and woman sat on either side of the hearth. A big black cat lay between them.

'You're the Irishman what killed my three sons,' said the old man.

'That's him,' the woman added.

'None other,' mewed the cat.

'You won't leave this castle until you fight me,' the old man shouted, jumping to his feet.

'And me.' The woman was on her feet too.

'Not to mention me,' squealed the cat.

The woman attacked first. She had steel spurs on her fingers for all the world like a fighting cock's. She scraped and tore at the lad's face and throat, but in the end he got the better of her and killed her.

On his hands, the old man wore rings with small blades welded into them. He raised these, but Seven Year Son sliced off his head before he could come within range.

When the cat stood up, a few tons of ashes dropped to the floor. Some of it went into the lad's eyes, blinding him temporarily. The cat stuck its tail into the fire and lit its tip. It scorched the eyes and ears of Seven Year Son. The fur stopped burning but not before it exposed an iron gaff. The cat whirled around the kitchen, describing an arc with its tail. This split Seven Year Son open from belly to neck.

Meanwhile, the daughter of the King of England was looking for him everywhere. When she came to the castle and saw the door open, she entered and came across the carnage. She wailed and keened and clung to the remains of Seven Year Son. One scream made the cat leap on to the mantelpiece with the fright. Noticing the movement, she looked up. There was a bottle beside the cat. She took it down and read its label:

Prescribed by the fear leighis of the sidhe. Can cure
carbuncle and palsy in goats or humans. Can cure
death itself if rubbed all over within an hour of demise.

Potion of a fairy doctor! Not believing her luck,
she massaged the lad with the oil. His gaping
wounds snapped closed and he hopped to his feet.
From the mantelpiece, the cat said, 'This time I
will kill you and the girl so that you won't rise a
second time.'

'There are no ashes on your back to help you
now,' shouted Seven Year Son, grabbing the Sword
of Strength and holding it at the ready. When the
cat tried the trick with its tail, Seven Year Son
caught it in mid air and sliced it up.

The daughter of the King of England ran to his
arms and kissed him. Then she led him through all
the rooms in the castle and each was a different
country. Oriental glades gave way to sea-washed
stretches of sand. Western skies blended with
magical northern lights and southern stars. There
were snow-covered hills, blazing sun and pasture.
The lad was enchanted at such beauty and the girl
took advantage of this.

'Couldn't you live here with me instead of
returning to Ireland? Am I not as attractive as the
daughter of your own country's king?'

Seven Year Son said he did not wish to offend,
but he explained that he had given his word and

must return. He gave the girl the keys, however, and told her to enjoy the wealth that they would bring. 'I have all I could wish for back home,' he added, 'and, never fear, you will find a man nearly as good as me sometime.' Even his vanity did not put her off, but she knew she would have to be resigned to losing him.

Well, that night, the king brought Seven Year Son to dinner in the palace. While they were eating, a stag appeared at the window. Seven Year Son almost retched when he saw what happened. The king opened the window and allowed the stag to defecate into his mouth. Appalled and disgusted, the Irish lad jumped to his feet and swore to kill the rude animal. The king said, 'Do no such thing. That stag comes here only when I have guests. It wishes to bring shame on me. But if you do not go home quickly, God knows what might happen to you. Seven years ago a stranger came here and asked for my daughter's hand. At supper, he reacted just like you. Next day, he and my two sons went hunting the stag. I have never seen them since.'

At breakfast, next morning, the stag came to the window again and the same disgusting procedure followed. It was too much for a clean-living Irish lad, so Seven Year Son left his royal fry and took off after the animal. The deer kept the same distance between them, but just as it was nearing its den, the Irish lad sprang through the air and landed near enough to draw blood with a swipe of his sword. The stag hobbled on and Seven Year Son followed it into a dark cave. When his eyes got used to the light, he saw a butcher carving up a live *banbh*. The poor young pig was squealing, so he had to shout to be heard.

'Did you see a dirty stag come in?'

'The only thing dirty I saw was yourself,' answered the butcher.

'Don't be so smart! Did you see anything come in?'

'Only yourself.'

'Well then, you must be the stag,' Seven Year Son shouted, as he lifted the butcher's apron. Sure enough, blood was dripping from his flank. 'Now, where are the three men who hunted you seven years ago?'

'They are upstairs, turned into stone. And if you cannot prove your manliness, you will become an ornamental pebble yourself,' said the stag.

'What proof do you want?'

'When this *banbh* is boiled, you must take him out of the pot with just the fork.'

That was no trouble to Seven Year Son. He lifted the pig, pot, crane and all with one hand. He then ordered the stag to go upstairs and return the men to their proper shapes. It did so and the boy told them to go back to the palace and be good to their father and sister. Then he turned to the stag, now restored to animal form. 'I will give you one chance. Go to the king's palace in the morning. I will follow you. If I do not catch you, you will be safe. If I do, you will die.'

Next morning the stag did indeed set off for the palace. Seven Year Son followed but, like before, could not gain any ground on it. As a result, the stag was already acting as before at the window when Seven Year Son caught up. He cut the head clean off the dirty creature. The king was delighted; more so when Seven Year Son told him that his two sons and prospective son-in-law were even then on their way home.

It took the others seven days — testimony to the agility of Seven Year Son. There was great jubilation and Seven Year Son waited until the suitor wed the King of England's daughter. Then he returned to Ireland and had another great day when he married the daughter of the King of Ireland. The couple, their parents, the English king, his daughter and her husband lived happily ever after. That makes seven!

FIFTEEN

A CORK BANSHEE

In times past, if a child found a rack or comb with broken teeth in a hedgerow, it brought anxiety to the heart. Terror, sometimes, because such an implement was, sure as God, a *cíor bean chaoint*, a keening woman's comb. In other words, it belonged to the *Morrígan*, the *badb* or, more commonly, the Banshee. This fairy woman followed certain families, mainly Gradys, Kavanaghs, O'Neills, O'Donnells and O'Briens. On the night before the member of a household died, she howled in the distance, the terrifying cry coming nearer as the moment of death approached.

A well-to-do Cork widower called Grady had one son, Henry, and three daughters, Angela, the youngest, Mary and Julie. When Grady died, his son joined the army, so his brother managed his estate and kept the girls in luxury. Privately taught, their music teacher was a violinist. This man, George Freeman, was of noble descent, but was a man-about-town and a compulsive gambler. He was forced to give lessons to repay some of his gambling debts. He infatuated the three girls with his superb music. Being the eldest, Julie felt she had the true right to become his beloved. This aroused the jealousy of Angela, who considered herself madly in love with the man.

Twenty-year-old Julie was a sleep-walker, and her uncle had devised numerous methods of keeping the mansion safe and of ensuring that his eldest daughter never left the house when asleep. For one thing, he had Mary share her bedroom and he tied the clothes of Julie's bed to hers, so that she would be alerted to any movement. The jealousy between Julie and Angela was developing into enmity when Mary went on holiday to Scotland. Consequently, when her uncle asked Angela to take Mary's place in Julie's bedroom, she begged to be excused. Being a doting uncle, he agreed.

The girls' governess, Beth, was reading to Angela one June evening. A red sun was sinking over the woodland that surrounded the estate, painting the manor lake red. Angela thought it a glorious sight, but the feeling of well-being it brought faded when Beth began to confide in her.

'You know, child, that the Banshee follows the Gradys. She wailed around this house before your dear mother died and, as for the night before your father passed away, God rest his soul, she was roaring like Doran's ass.'

Beth was inclined to scoff, but noticed the concern in the old lady's eyes, and listened intently.

'I'm as worried as a clocking hen these two days past, because on Monday night I heard the very same cry. Your brother and sister are in foreign parts and who knows what might have happened

to them, God between us and all harm.' Just then
the postman arrived, bearing a letter from Mary in
which she told Angela about the great time she was
having. It helped to ease Angela's anxiety, but Beth's
information preyed on her mind all day, and when
she went to bed that night she prayed for her
family as she had never done before. She prayed
and prayed and finally dropped off to sleep.

Wakening a few hours later, she heard the
village clock striking two. The moon was casting a
pale wash through net curtains that were moving
slightly in a gentle breeze. So a floral outline moved
along her counterpane and across the floor. The
design seemed to gather into the shape of a woman
and when the breeze lessened, it floated towards the
window. A cloud then scurried across the moon and
the shadow disappeared. Angela knew she should
not be afraid, but something prompted her to get
out of bed and look out. Just as she did, the cloud
parted and the moon shone down on the woodland
and lake. What Angela saw stuck her to the floor in
terror. A woman was standing in her uncle's boat,
her hands outstretched. She appeared like the
outline Angela had seen in her room earlier, but was
fully formed and clad in a white nightgown. It was
Julie. She bent at the waist, untied the mooring
rope and the boat began to leave the shore.

Throwing on a gown, cloak and shoes, Angela
sped downstairs, out across the lawn, through the

orchard and on towards the mooring platform. Another cloud crossed the moon and plunged the place into darkness. Angela tripped over an oak root and hit her head off the mighty trunk. She cried out in pain and thought she heard an answering wail from the woodland. It became louder and then changed into an evil cackle before dropping suddenly and becoming an almost soothing keen. Then the moon reappeared.

The boat was rocking gently a few yards from the shore. Its keel lay across Julie's waist. Weeds and sedge held her head and feet under the water, while her nightgown rose and dropped on the rippling surface. Angela gave a low moan of grief and fainted.

Meanwhile, George Freeman was up early and setting off for a morning's hunting. He was riding past the wood when he heard either the Banshee's cry or Angela's. He spurred his horse in that direction and soon came across the tragic sight. He carried Angela to the house and alerted the servants, who then attended to Julie's corpse. Mary Grady came home in time for the funeral but nobody could trace the whereabouts of Henry, who by that time had left the army.

Two years later, poor Beth was dead and Angela still loved George Freeman. He visited the house regularly but she never told him of her feelings.

Mary was reminiscing with her sister one evening. The two girls were laughing over some childhood memories when Mary jumped to her feet with a startled look on her face.

'That wailing, Angela. Do you hear it?'

'I hear nothing but the song of the thrush in the orchard,' Angela answered, and Mary fell back into her chair in a faint. When she recovered she told Angela that she had heard the Banshee's cry again. Although she did not admit it, Angela was terrified. Almost immediately, they heard hurried footsteps on the stairs. A servant knocked and entered.

'Mr Gray's footman is waiting below, Miss Mary. He has a coach and four outside and says his master is expecting you and Miss Angela.'

The girls could not understand this. They had never met Mr Gray, who had arrived in the locality from England during the past year. Neighbours had reported that he was quiet and retiring and was in ill-health. They questioned the footman as to the reason for the request, but he could only say that his master had said it was a matter of great urgency. Both ladies dressed and went to Mr Gray's home. The footman brought them upstairs to his master's bedroom. A grave-faced doctor stood by the bed in which lay a wasted, sickly man. Only when he spoke did the ladies realise that this Mr Gray was their brother Henry. In barely audible words, he told them of his years in the army, where he was penniless, and out of it, when he accumulated great wealth. Mary and Angela wept when he said that he missed his home terribly but was afraid that nobody would forgive him or allow him to enter his old home. 'So I bought this house, left the 'd' out of my surname and posed as Mr Gray. All the time, I watched my dear sisters from afar. I prayed for their welfare.'

He smiled weakly, then lay back and died. A will disclosed that he left all his wealth to Mary and Angela.

The Banshee had heralded the death of another Grady. Angela was disturbed and miserable. More so the following year, when George Freeman married Mary Grady. Angela never revealed her love for him. She remained single for life.

SIXTEEN

THE BALL IN DONEGAL

Twenty years old and single, Manus McGilligan was searching for a lost ewe in Donegal's Bluestack Mountains one day. He did not realise how late in the evening it was until the sun sank and he was left in darkness. Unable to find his way home, he lay down under a lone bush on a mossy ridge. It was a fairy thorn. He fell asleep, but almost immediately a well-dressed, handsome man awakened him and invited him to a ball which Lord Barnes Mór was giving. Manus had never heard of such a man but, being a lively lad and game for diversion, he agreed immediately.

The gentleman walked him through sweet-smelling fields of flowers and fruit. Birds with multicoloured plumage sang in the trees. They passed by streams where silver salmon leaped and glistened in the warm glow of a golden sunset. Manus felt at peace.

His escort led him up a red-gravelled avenue to a large blue castle, the biggest building Manus had ever seen. It had fifty chimneys and a hundred windows and each of its ten doors was as high as Errigal Mountain. A footman opened the widest of these and they entered. Servants in braided livery rushed hither and thither, bearing salvers of viands. One noticed the couple arriving. He came over and bowed, smiled to Manus's escort and led the way up an ivory staircase.

'Meet Lord Barnes Mór. My lord, this is Mister Manus McGilligan.' The young man made the introductions.

'Welcome to my castle!' the tall man said. 'Pray, join in the feasting and dancing.'

Manus became embarrassed. 'I'm not in my blue Sunday suit, sir. How could I join all these fine people dressed up like bushes at holy wells,' he said. Lord Barnes Mór smiled and told a servant to bring Manus away to his own room and dress him appropriately.

The walls of the lord's room were lined with ebony-framed mirrors. Crystal chandeliers hung from a gilt roof, surely a hundred of them, because the room was two miles long. Footmen came to attend Manus. They tried on green suits, blue cloaks, yellow waistcoats and white knickerbockers, but he spotted a crimson costume with lace trimmings and said he liked it. He put it on and felt very self-confident. A bell rang and a butler directed him to the ballroom. Such opulence he never could have imagined, let alone witness, back in his hillside townland. As he descended a flight of marble steps his escort announced, 'My lords, dukes, barons, ladies and other folk, allow me to present to you Mister Manus McGilligan who will honour you with his company for the evening.' Everybody bowed and Manus felt very important altogether.

Then all the beautiful ladies in magnificent dresses looked his way and he winked at two of them. They rushed over to him and began fighting about who would dance with him. As they argued, another young lady took his arm and began to waltz. Never had he heard such lovely music, although there were no musicians. It seemed to come from beneath the floor. Also, he realised that, although he had never danced anything but a reel or a jig, he was waltzing better than the most elegant gentleman on the floor. The night went on and one lovely lady after another asked him to dance.

The men began to get jealous and one tried to trip Manus during a minuet. His partner chastised him and asked Manus for the next dance. She told the other women what had happened and they all left their menfolk and lined up waiting their turn for a dance with Manus. He did polkas and quadrilles to beat the band (even though there was none). Such grace and litheness were never seen. The attention and the exertion were too much, however, and before half the line of applicants received dances, Manus collapsed.

'I'm exhausted, ladies,' he apologised. He looked out the door of the ballroom and saw servants with piles of roast quail passing by. Only then did he realise that he had not eaten since breakfast and that he was ravenous. He winked at the women and said, 'Maybe now if you gave me something to eat, I might recover some of my strength and give a few more of you a whirl.'

'Oh yes! Oh yes!' called the ladies. 'Give him some quail.'

'Oh no! Oh no!' called Lord Barnes Mór. 'We must have a tale.' He turned to the ladies. 'Shame on you. You all know the rules of this castle.' Then he explained to Manus that before he ate he must tell the assembled company a story.

'A story!' laughed Manus. 'I never told a story in my life. I have no stories.'

Lord Barnes Mór frowned. 'No story? What sort of an Irishman are you that cannot make up a story? Well, I'm afraid I have bad news for you, my lad. No tale, no quail. We here frown on people who cannot amuse us with a saga or two. And I might add that we think such a numbskull is useless to man, beast or bullock. I'm afraid you will have to leave us.' With that, the servant who had attended to him all evening placed his little finger under Manus's knee and tossed him out the window as if he were a feather.

Downhearted and alone, Manus made his way down the red avenue. At its gate he came across three undertakers who were trying without much success to lift a coffin. 'We need a fourth man under the tail and here's the very fellow. Slap your shoulder under this, Manus, for you know it is one of the works of mercy to bury the dead.' Manus obliged and soon they reached a cemetery. They put down the coffin and told Manus to dig a grave. He thought this a bit unfair but, although still very tired and hungry, he cut the sod and dug one. When it was ready, they began to lower the coffin, but a voice called from below. 'Shame on you for disturbing my poor father's skeleton. Fill up this hole immediately and bury your dead somewhere else.'

Manus said he was sorry, filled up the hole and dug another a few feet away. Again, when he had finished, he heard the voice. 'Shame on you for disturbing my poor sister's skeleton. Fill up this hole immediately and bury your dead somewhere else.'

By the time he had completed the third grave, Manus was in a state of utter exhaustion. He and the three undertakers began to lower the coffin, but the voice called again. 'Shame on you for disturbing my poor mother's skeleton. Fill up this hole immediately and bury your dead somewhere else.'

Well, the owner of the voice must have had a large extended family, for Manus dug grave after grave and was derided for disturbing skeletons of brothers, cousins, aunts, uncles, grandparents, godparents and half-sisters twice removed. His hands were peeling and the raw flesh pained him intensely. He buckled at the knees and his back ached. Perspiration rolled off him until the undertakers had to bale out every grave with a bucket.

Then Manus had an idea. He dug a grave five feet six inches, half a foot less than the others. He was hoping that the owner of the voice had no midgets in the family as he and the others lowered the coffin. He held his breath and waited for the voice, but none came. Lowering the remains, he was so relieved that he let the rope slide through his hands too quickly. The coffin hit the edge of the grave at an angle and the lid popped off. Manus looked inside and screamed. It was the corpse of Manus McGilligan.

'I knew I was dead tired, but this is the dickens entirely,' he screamed, before taking to his heels

like a scalded cat. The three undertakers followed
him and dragged him back. Despite his fatigue, he
struggled and fought for an hour and a minute and
began to get the better of the others. Then he saw
one of them draw a fairy wand from under his
cloak. As fast as a happy dog's tail he weaved and
ducked and snatched the rod. Then he tapped each
man with it and one by one they dropped dead.

Away with Manus to the castle then. The
servant who had attended to him when he arrived
first was at the door. He took Manus to the
bathroom. Three young girls washed him from
head to foot. Manus was embarrassed, but he felt
refreshed and not at all tired. Back to Lord Barnes
Mór's room then for more fittings. Footmen
dressed him in an outfit even more elegant than
before. This time they carried him to the ballroom
in a golden sedan-chair that was upholstered in
satin and decorated with rare gems and trinkets.
Everybody was dancing as spiritedly as if the ball
were only beginning. One by one the ladies
noticed him and three by three they left their
menfolk and surged forward to meet him. But
Lord Barnes Mór halted them and confronted
Manus.

'You said you had no story to tell. Why then
should you dare return?'

'Will you sit down there, your lordship, and
not be getting your periwig in knots. I have a story

to unfold, the like of which you wouldn't hear in a month of Sundays and half an hour.'

'Very well then, take the throne.'

So Manus McGilligan sat on the fairy throne and began his story. No *seanchaí*, no orator, no bishop, pastor, abbot or politician ever received such attention. Men held their breaths and women their hearts as words tumbled from Manus like waters from a cataract. At the end there was a moment of absolute silence, then a deafening clamour. It rattled windows and doors until crows in rookeries ten miles away awoke and gannets in the Saltee Islands thought there was another fair in Wexford. The fairy host clapped and cheered and Lord Barnes Mór came to Manus, shook his hand and said, 'I know I am only 1,000 years old, but never before have I heard such a mighty tale. And if I live another millenium, I know I will never hear the likes again.' Then he turned to the servants and said, 'Tend to this man as if he were the King of Ireland, the King of Spain and the King of France all wrapped up together. Nothing that we can provide is too good for him.'

Before the servants could respond, the women surrounded Manus and carried him shoulder-high to the banqueting room. They fed him the choicest sections of quail and other dishes and filled his glass repeatedly with the oldest and most expensive wine. When he could eat no more they carried him to a bedroom. They placed him on a bed dressed in gold-trimmed silk brocade. It was softer than anything he had ever felt before. One lady entered with a harp. She played the most exquisite music and in no time at all Manus fell asleep.

He awoke, but instead of looking into the eyes of a fairy harpist he was peering into the pupils of his lost ewe. The sun was shining down from above Barnesmore gap (Manus thought that name had a familiar ring to it). Then he remembered all that had happened. He was a little sad when he realised that he would enjoy no more of the high life that the Donegal fairies had given him. But he shook himself, stood up and began to guide the lost ewe back to his farm. In the farmyard he saw his spade where he had left it. Its handle was covered with blood and tiny pieces of flesh. Manus shook his head in wonder. He decided that life was good after all.

I'll never have to buy another drink as long as I have this story to tell, he said to himself. And he never did— until he moved south to Sligo, where they do not appreciate good storytelling!